THE MEXICAN POLITICAL SYSTEM IN TRANSITION

THE MEXICAN POLITICAL SYSTEM IN TRANSITION

WAYNE A. CORNELIUS
and
ANN L. CRAIG

Printed with the assistance of the Tinker Foundation

Monograph Series, 35
Center for U.S.-Mexican Studies
University of California, San Diego
1991

Printed in the United States of America by
the Center for U.S.-Mexican Studies
University of California, San Diego

Cover photo: PRI presidential candidate Carlos Salinas de
Gortari campaigns in Mexico, 1988. Photo courtesy of the
Partido Revolucionario Institucional.

ISBN: 1-878367-04-8

CONTENTS

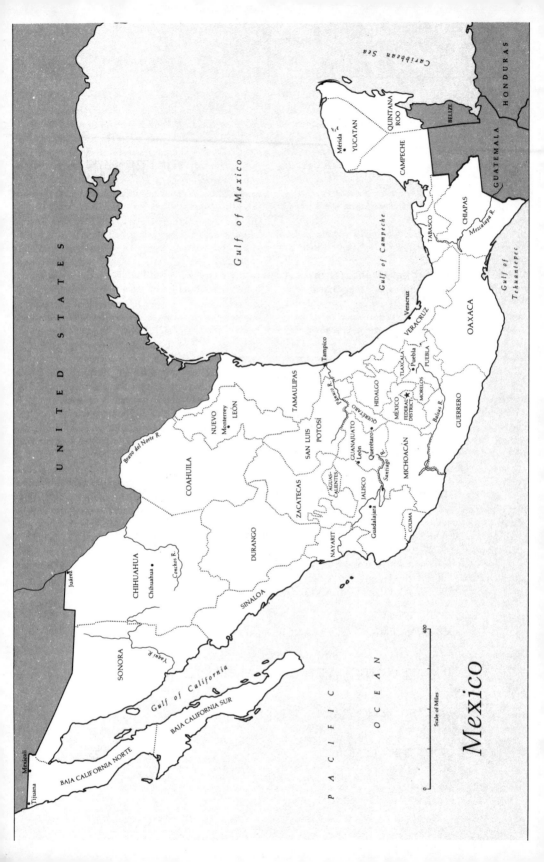

The Mexican Political System: The End of an Era

On July 7, 1988, Mexico's newly elected president, Carlos Salinas de Gortari, appeared before the television cameras to make a startling pronouncement: "The era of the virtual one-party system [in Mexico] has ended," giving way to a period of "intense political competition." Salinas's statement was intended both as a celebration of Mexico's maturing political system and as a thinly veiled warning to the leadership of his own party, the Partido Revolucionario Institucional (PRI), which had dominated all levels of the political system continuously since its creation in 1929. Henceforth, PRI leaders would be operating in a much more fluid and uncertain political environment. Given the strength demonstrated by opposition parties, the government could no longer guarantee the outcomes of the electoral process.

Although many PRI militants were clearly unpersuaded that the era of one-party dominance had ended, the results of the July 6 election vividly reflected the new political realities of which Salinas spoke: For the first time in history, a Mexican president had been elected with less than half of the votes cast (48.7 percent)— more than 20 percentage points below the vote share attributed to PRI presidential candidate Miguel de la Madrid in the 1982 election.[1] Also for the first time, a PRI presidential candidate had failed to carry several whole states: Baja California Norte, México State, Michoacán, Morelos, and the Federal District, which includes most of the Mexico City metropolitan area. These five entities were won by ex-PRIista Cuauhtémoc Cárdenas, who was officially credited

---

[1] If the 695,042 annulled ballots and 14,333 votes cast for nonregistered presidential candidates in the 1988 election are *excluded* from the percentage base, Salinas's share rises to a bare majority (50.74 percent). If these votes are *included* in the tally, Salinas becomes the first Mexican president elected only by a plurality of the total votes cast.

with 31.1 percent of the nationwide vote—far more than any previous opposition candidate.

The ruling party's control of the Congress was weakened significantly, setting the stage for a new era in executive-legislative relations. Sixty-six PRI candidates for seats in the lower house of Congress were defeated—nearly as many as the total of ruling party candidates defeated in all elections between 1946 and 1985. For the 1988-91 period, the PRI was reduced to a bare working majority in the Chamber of Deputies (260 out of 500 seats), and for the first time since the ruling party was founded in 1929, opposition party candidates were elected to the Senate (4 out of 64 seats). Because the PRI no longer commanded a two-thirds majority in the lower house, President Salinas would have to negotiate with the opposition party delegations to secure passage of key legislation amending the Constitution.

Moreover, the Congress had ceased to function as a reliable instrument for the internal distribution of power and its perks within the ruling party. With the recognition of so many opposition victories for congressional seats in 1988, aspiring PRIistas had to face the reality that nomination by their party was no longer tantamount to election. The tradition of the *"carro completo"* (clean sweep) by PRI candidates was clearly threatened.

What happened after the 1988 election was nearly as extraordinary as the election results themselves. The validity of the presidential results was immediately challenged by all opposition parties, which alleged massive fraud by the PRI and government election officials and refused to recognize the legitimacy of the Salinas government.[2] During the three-month period between the election and certification of the results by the newly elected Congress acting as the Electoral College, Mexico would endure unprecedented uncertainty about whether the newly elected

---

[2]The actual extent of irregularities in the tabulation of the 1988 presidential election will never be determined. Within a few hours after the polls closed, a "computer crash" in the National Registry of Voters allegedly interrupted the count, days would pass before even preliminary results for a majority of the places were announced. No "exit" surveys of voters leaving by the government. In subsequent months, govern o a large portion of the sealed ballot boxes that had ertheless, the official tally for Salinas was within a few wing in several of the most scientific preelection polls ncuestas y los resultados oficiales," *Perfil de La Jornada*, etailed analyses of the partial, publicly released election concluded that Salinas probably did win, but that his denas was considerably smaller than the nineteen-point ficial results.

president would be able to assume office or whether the election results would be annulled by the Congress in response to massive protest demonstrations led by a coalition of opposition parties. In the end, the opposition pulled back from its confrontational, anti-system strategy. Salinas's election was certified, but only with the votes of PRI members of Congress; not a single opposition party representative supported his confirmation.

Mexico's political earthquake of 1988 produced significant shifts in well-established patterns of electoral behavior. The emergence of a left-of-center, nonsocialist opposition movement outside of the ruling party, led by the son of Lázaro Cárdenas, Mexico's most revered president of the postrevolutionary era, undermined the PRI's electoral base in the most developed, urbanized parts of the country while cutting into its formerly "safe" support in rural areas. The neo-Cardenista coalition drew relatively little support away from the Partido de Acción Nacional (PAN), Mexico's principal right-of-center opposition party, which held its own in its traditional strongholds. The strong performance of opposition candidates of both right and left in several of the states where gubernatorial or municipal elections were held in 1989 proved that the previous year's results were no fluke. The PRI's sixty-year-old monopoly of state governorships was finally broken, with the overwhelming, officially recognized victory of PANista candidate Ernesto Ruffo in Baja California Norte. Finally, the low turnout in the 1988 presidential election (less than half of those eligible bothered to vote) and considerably lower turnout rates in most state and local elections held during 1989 and 1990 signaled a serious erosion of public confidence in the whole system of parties and elections.

Only a decade ago, such drastic changes in the Mexican political system would have seemed unthinkable. This regime had been the most stable in the modern history of Latin America, with a well-earned reputation for resilience, flexibility, and a high capacity for co-optation of dissidents. In the early 1970s concerns had been raised about the stability of the system, after the bloody repression of a student protest movement in Mexico City by President Gustavo Díaz Ordaz on the eve of the 1968 Olympic Games. Many analysts at that time suggested that Mexico was entering a period of "institutional crisis," requiring fundamental reforms in both political arrangements and economic development strategy. But the discovery of massive oil and natural gas resources during the last half of the decade gave the incumbent regime a new lease on life. The continued support of masses and elites could be purchased with an apparently limitless supply of "petro-pesos," even without major structural reforms. The government's room for maneuver was abruptly erased by the collapse of the oil boom in August 1982, due to a combination of adverse international economic circumstances (falling oil prices, rising interest rates, recession in the United States) and fiscally irresponsible domestic policies. Real wages and living standards for the vast majority of Mexicans plummeted, and the government committed itself to a socially painful restructuring of the economy, including a drastic shrinkage of the sector owned and managed by the government itself.

The economic crisis of the 1980s, unprecedented in depth and duration, placed enormous stress on Mexico's political system. Indeed, it could be argued that the serious divisions that emerged within the political elite in 1987-88 and the PRI's electoral debacles of 1988-89 were inevitable consequences of the multiple failures of government performance in managing the economy. It does not necessarily follow, however, that a recovery of economic health in the 1990s will reverse the decline of Mexico's hegemonic one-party regime. The PRI has managed to regain some of the electoral ground that it lost in 1988, but its image of invincibility has been shattered.

The 1988 election results demonstrated beyond all reasonable doubt that the political system put in place by Lázaro Cárdenas in the 1930s has outlived its usefulness. In many ways, Mexican society—increasingly complex and heterogeneous, more urban, better educated, rapidly being integrated into the world economy—has simply outgrown that system. The main issues now are what set of political structures and arrangements will replace it, how rapidly the change will occur, and how conflictual the transition process will be.

Historical Perspective

LEGACIES OF COLONIALISM

Long before Hernán Cortés landed in 1519 and began the Spanish conquest of Mexico, its territory was inhabited by numerous Indian civilizations. Of these, the Maya in the Yucatán peninsula and the Toltec on the central plateau had developed the most complex political and economic organization. Both of these civilizations had disintegrated, however, before the Spaniards arrived. Smaller Indian societies were decimated by diseases introduced by the invaders or were vanquished by the sword. Subsequent grants of land and Indian labor by the Spanish Crown to the colonists further isolated the rural Indian population and deepened their exploitation.

The combined effects of attrition, intermarriage, and cultural penetration of Indian regions have drastically reduced the proportion of Mexico's population culturally identified as Indian. By 1990, according to census figures, only 8.5 percent of the population spoke an Indian language.[3] The Indian minority has been persistently marginal to the national economy and political system. Today, the indigenous population is heavily concentrated in areas that the government classifies as the country's most economically depressed, located primarily in the southeast and the center of the country. They engage in rainfall-dependent subsistence agriculture using traditional methods of cultivation, are seasonally employed as migrant laborers in commercial agriculture, or produce crafts for sale in regional and national markets. The Indian population is an especially troubling reminder of the millions of people who have been left behind by uneven development in twentieth-century Mexico.

---

[3]This represents an undercount, since the census counts only Indians over the age of five. Indians constitute an estimated 15 percent of the total population.

The importance of Spain's colonies in the New World lay in their ability to provide the Crown with vital resources to fuel the Spanish economy. Mexico's mines provided gold and silver in abundance until the wars of independence began in 1810. After independence, Mexico continued to export these ores, supplemented in subsequent eras by hemp, cotton, textiles, oil, and winter vegetables.

The Crown expected the colony to produce enough basic food crops for its own sustenance. Agriculture developed—unevenly—alongside the resource-exporting sectors of the economy. Some farming was small-scale subsistence agriculture. Most large landholdings in the colonial era were farmed through combinations of sharecropping, debt peonage, and large-scale cultivation; they produced basic food grains and livestock for regional markets. Over the nineteenth century, some large landholders made significant capital investments in machinery to process agricultural products (grain mills and textile factories) and in agricultural inputs (land, dams, and improved livestock). These agricultural entrepreneurs produced commercial crops for the national or international market. Today, the relationship between subsistence agriculture on tiny plots (*minifundia*) and large-scale, highly mechanized commercial agriculture is far more complex; but the extreme dualism and erratic performance that characterize Mexico's agriculture sector are among the most important bottlenecks in the country's economic development.

CHURCH AND STATE

Since the Spanish conquest, the Roman Catholic church has been an institution of enduring power in Mexico, but the nature of its power has changed notably in the postcolonial era. Priests joined the Spanish invaders in an evangelical mission to promote conversion of the Indians to Catholicism, and individual priests have continued to play important roles in national history. Father Miguel Hidalgo y Costilla helped launch Mexico's war of independence in 1810, and Father José María Morelos y Pavón replaced Hidalgo as spiritual and military leader of the independence movement when Hidalgo was executed by the Crown in 1811.

During Mexico's postindependence period, institutional antagonisms between church and central government have occasionally flared into open confrontations on such issues as church wealth, educational policy, the content of public school textbooks, and political activism by the church. The Constitutions of 1857 and 1917 formally established the separation of church and state and defined their respective domains. Constitutional provisions dramatically reduced the church's power and wealth by national-izing its property, including large agricultural landholdings. The 1917 Constitution makes church-affiliated schools subject to the authority of the federal government, denies priests the right to vote or speak publicly on political issues, and gives the govern-ment the right to limit the number of priests who can serve in Mexico.

Government efforts during the 1920s to enforce these constitu-tional provisions led the church to suspend religious services throughout the country. Church leaders also supported the Cris-tero rebellion of 1927-29, as a last stand against the incursions of a centralizing state. Large landholders took advantage of the con-flict, inciting devout peasants to take up arms against local dissi-dents who had begun to petition the government for land reform. Because the church also opposed redistribution of land, the land-owners could depict themselves as faithful partners in the holy war against a state that espoused such policies. The rebellion caused 100,000 combatant deaths, uncounted civilian casualties, and economic devastation in a large part of central Mexico. The settlement of the conflict established, once and for all, the church's subordination to the state, in return for which the government relaxed its restrictions on church activities in nonpolitical arenas.

This accord inaugurated a long period of relative tranquility in church-state relations, during which many of the anticlerical pro-visions of the 1917 Constitution (such as the prohibition on church involvement in education) were ignored by both the government and the church. The central church hierarchy—among the most conservative in Latin America—cooperated with the government on a variety of issues, and the church posed no threat to the official party's hegemony.

Today the church retains considerable influence, particularly in Mexico's rural areas and small cities. But even though more than 80 percent of the country's population identify themselves as Catholics in sample surveys, this religious preference does not translate automatically into support for the church's positions on social or political issues. Formal church opposition to birth control, for example, has not prevented widespread adoption of family planning practices in Mexico since the government launched a birth control program in the mid-1970s. Nevertheless, the govern-ment respects and perhaps even fears the Catholic church's capac-ity for mass mobilization, which was demonstrated dramatically during Pope John Paul II's visits to Mexico in 1979 and 1990. On each of those occasions, an estimated 20 million Mexicans participated in street demonstrations and other public gatherings held in connection with the papal visit. In 1990, a well-organized protest movement organized by the Catholic church in response to a state law legalizing abortions in the southern state of Chiapas succeeded in overturning the law, virtually ending hopes for liberalization of abortion laws throughout Mexico. The Catholic church has also been able to enlist the help of the federal government and the PRI in its drive to prevent the growth of evangelical Protestant "sects" in Mexico.

During the 1980s church-state relations were strained by the highly visible political activism of some church leaders in northern Mexico, who publicly criticized electoral fraud committed by the PRI and sided openly with the conservative opposition party, the Partido de Acción Nacional (PAN). In 1986, the archbishop of the state of Chihuahua ordered the temporary suspension of all church services, in protest of the fraud-ridden elections of July 1986 in his state. This and other episodes of overt political activism by church leaders and priests led the government in December 1986 to amend the federal electoral code to provide stiff fines and jail terms of up to seven years for clergy found to take sides in electoral campaigns.

In 1988 President Salinas began an unprecedented formal rapprochement with the church, as part of his project to "modernize" Mexican politics and win back some of the proclerical PAN's supporters for the official party. He invited several senior church leaders to attend his inauguration, met with the pope during his visit to Mexico in 1990, and took the first steps toward establishing full diplomatic relations with the Vatican. Salinas was aware of the considerable public support for changes that would close the formal breech between church and state. Opinion polls show that a majority of Mexicans in large cities favors granting priests the same political rights as other citizens, including the right to vote in elections. By a smaller margin, the public is willing to allow private schools to teach religion. The average Mexican still has reservations, however, about lifting restrictions on political and economic activities by the church as an institution.[4]

REVOLUTION AND ITS AFTERMATH

The civil conflict that erupted in Mexico in 1910 is often referred to as the first of the great "social revolutions" that shook the world early in the twentieth century, but Mexico's upheaval originated

---

[4]See, for example, "Encuestalía: ¿Quién quiere un Papa?" *Nexos* 148 (April 1990).

within the country's ruling class. The Revolution did not begin as a spontaneous uprising of the common people against an entrenched dictator, Porfirio Díaz, and against the local bosses and landowners who exploited them. Even though hundreds of thousands of workers and peasants ultimately participated in the civil strife, most of the revolutionary leadership came from the younger generation of middle- and upper-class Mexicans who had become disenchanted with three and a half decades of increasingly heavy-handed rule by the aging dictator and his clique. These disgruntled members of the elite saw their future opportunities for economic and political mobility blocked by the closed group surrounding Díaz.

Led by Francisco I. Madero, whose family had close ties with the ruling group, these liberal bourgeois reformers were committed to opening up the political system and creating new opportunities for themselves within a capitalist economy whose basic features they did not challenge. They sought not to destroy the established order but rather to make it work more in their own interest than that of the foreign capitalists who had come to dominate key sectors of Mexico's economy during the Porfirian dictatorship (a period called "the Porfiriato").

Of course, some serious grievances had accumulated among workers and peasants. Once the rebellion against Díaz got under way, leaders who appealed to the disadvantaged masses pressed their claims against the central government. Emiliano Zapata led a movement of peasants in the state of Morelos who were bent on regaining the land they had lost to the rural aristocracy by subterfuge during the Porfiriato. In the north, Pancho Villa led an army consisting of jobless workers, small landowners, and cattle hands, whose main interest was steady employment. As the various revolutionary leaders contended for control of the central government, the political order that had been created and enforced by Díaz disintegrated into warlordism—powerful regional gangs led by revolutionary caudillos (political-military strongmen) who aspired more to increasing their personal wealth and social status than to leading a genuine social revolution. In sum, "although class conflict was central to the Revolution, the Revolution cannot be reduced to class conflict....[It] was a mix of different classes, interests, and ideologies," giving rise to a state that enjoyed considerable autonomy vis-à-vis specific class interests.[5]

---

[5]Alan Knight, "Revolutionary Project, Recalcitrant People: Mexico, 1910-1940," in *The Revolutionary Process in Mexico: Essays on Political and Social Change, 1880-1940*, ed. Jaime E. Rodríguez (Los Angeles: UCLA Latin American Center, 1990), 228-29.

The first decade of the Revolution produced a new, remarkably progressive constitution, replacing the Constitution of 1857. The young middle-class elite that dominated the constitutional convention of 1916-17 "had little if any direct interest in labor unions or land distribution. But it was an elite that recognized the need for social change.... By 1916, popular demands for land and labor reform were too great to ignore."[6] Many historians today stress the continuities between prerevolutionary and postrevolutionary Mexico. The processes of economic modernization, capital accumulation, state building, and political centralization that gained considerable momentum during the Porfiriato were interrupted by civil strife from 1910 to 1920, but they resumed once a semblance of order had been restored. During the 1920s, the central government set out to eliminate or undermine the most powerful and independent-minded regional caudillos by co-opting the local power brokers (known traditionally as caciques). These local political bosses became, in effect, appendages of the central government, supporting its policies and maintaining control over the population in their communities. By the end of this period, leaders with genuine popular followings like Zapata and Villa had been assassinated, and control had been seized by a new postrevolutionary elite bent upon demobilizing the masses and establishing the hegemony of the central government.

The rural aristocracy of the Porfiriato had been weakened but not eliminated; its heirs still controlled large concentrations of property and other forms of wealth in many parts of the country. Most of the large urban firms that operated during the Porfiriato also survived, further demonstrating that the Revolution was not an attack on private capital per se.[7]

---

[6]Peter H. Smith, "The Making of the Mexican Constitution," in *The History of Parliamentary Behavior*, ed. William O. Aydelotte (Princeton, N.J.: Princeton University Press, 1977), 219. The Constitution of 1917 established the principle of state control over all natural resources, subordination of the church to the state, the government's right to redistribute land, and rights for labor that had not yet been secured even by the labor movement in the United States. Nearly two decades passed, however, before most of these constitutional provisions began to be implemented.

[7]Stephen Haber, *Industry and Underdevelopment: The Industrialization of Mexico, 1890-1940* (Stanford, Calif.: Stanford University Press, 1988). This helps to explain why, despite the great violence of the 1910-20 period and the destruction of the political and military institutions of the Porfirian regime, the Mexican Revolution brought about so little in the way of immediate social reforms. More than twenty years would pass, for example, before large-scale redistribution of landholdings would begin, under President Lázaro Cárdenas.

THE CÁRENAS UPHEAVAL

Elite control was maintained during the 1930s, but this was nevertheless an era of massive social and political upheaval in Mexico. During the presidency of Lázaro Cárdenas (1934-40), peasants and urban workers succeeded for the first time in pressing their claims for land and higher wages; in fact, Cárdenas actively encouraged them to do so. The result was an unprecedented wave of strikes, protest demonstrations, and petitions for breaking up large rural estates.

Most disputes between labor and management during this period were settled, under government pressure, in favor of the workers. The Cárdenas administration also redistributed more than twice as much land as that expropriated by all of Cárdenas's predecessors since 1915, when Mexico's land reform program was formally initiated. By 1940 the country's land tenure system had been fundamentally altered, breaking the traditional domination of the large haciendas and creating a large sector of small peasant farmers called *ejidatarios*—more than 1.5 million of them—who had received plots of land under the agrarian reform program. The Cárdenas government actively encouraged the formation of new organizations of peasants and urban workers, grouped the new organizations into nationwide confederations, and provided arms to rural militias formed by the ejidatarios who had received plots of land (ejidos) from the government. Even Mexico's foreign relations were disrupted in 1938 when the Cárdenas government nationalized oil companies that had been operating in Mexico under U.S. and British ownership.

How do we explain this burst of reformism coming from a regime that since 1917 had grown increasingly conservative, aligned with U.S. and other foreign capitalists, and unresponsive to the accumulated grievances of Mexico's poor? Apparently Cárdenas and his followers took the interests of peasants and urban workers more seriously. They believed that the state could and should control both capital and labor, and that more vigorous state intervention on the side of the working classes could ameliorate the worst excesses of the capitalist economic system while preempting threats to political stability that might stem from neglect of the poor. Cárdenas's efforts to mobilize and organize the working classes were a necessary instrument of reform. Government-sponsored worker organizations were preferable to uncontrolled mass mobilization, and they were also an effective counterweight to the regular military and other conservative groups that resisted redistributive policies and that might even have tried to stage a coup to remove the Cardenistas from power. The organization of militant mass support groups that were tied directly to the Cárdenas administration made the cost of any such coup much higher than it would have been in their absence.

The Cárdenas era proved to be a genuine aberration in the development of postrevolutionary Mexico. Never before or since had the fundamental "who benefits?" question been addressed with such energy and commitment by a Mexican government. Mexican intellectuals frequently refer to 1938 as the high-water mark of the Mexican Revolution as measured by social progress, and characterize the period since then as a retrogression. Certainly, the distributive and especially the *re*distributive performance of the Mexican government declined sharply in the decades that followed, and the worker and peasant organizations formed during the Cárdenas era atrophied and became less and less likely to contest either the will of the government or the interests of Mexico's private economic elites. De facto reconcentration of landholdings and other forms of wealth occurred as the state provided increasingly generous support to the country's new commercial, industrial, and financial elites during a period of rapid industrialization.

Critics of the Cárdenas administration have laid much of the blame for this outcome on the kind of mass political organizing that occurred under Cárdenas. The resulting organizations were captives of the regime—tied so closely to it that they had no capacity for autonomous action. Under the control of a new group of national political leaders whose values and priorities were unfavorable to the working classes, these same organizations, after Cárdenas, functioned only to enforce political stability and limit lower-class demands for government benefits.

Although it is true that Cárdenas never really departed from the established tradition of paternalistic mobilization from above, there is substantial evidence that the revolutionary potential of the Mexican working class had been blunted long before Cárdenas assumed the presidency. Most peasants wanted mainly to become small independent landowners, being their own bosses rather than working as peons for exploitative hacienda owners. Like most of the urban workers who supported the Cárdenas regime, these campesinos did not have a national political agenda. They were able and willing for a few years to confront the "big capitalists" and those sectors of the state allied with them, but this was due in no small part to the encouragement and protection that they received from the national and state-level political leaders who were allied with Cárdenas.

During his last two years in office, Cárdenas himself backed away from a full-scale confrontation with domestic and foreign capitalists and moderated his redistributive policies. The changes introduced by his government had generated so much tension that a counterreform movement—led by a conservative military man and drawing support both from elites whose interests had been damaged by Cárdenas's policies and from disadvantaged groups who had not yet benefited from the reform programs—threatened the survival of his administration. To protect and consolidate the gains made for peasants and urban workers under his regime, Cárdenas moved to limit political polarization and prevent open class warfare.

Cárdenas represented a coalition of forces that was progressive but not committed to destroying the foundations of Mexican capitalism. While he was advised by left-wing Keynesian economists trained in England, Cárdenas himself was not a socialist. Cárdenas may have considered socialism a desirable long-term goal, but neither he nor his associates believed it was a realistic possibility for the immediate future.[8]

THE LEGACY OF REVOLUTION

What difference did it make, then, that beginning in 1910 Mexico suffered three decades of civil strife, political turmoil, and economic dislocation? Many contemporary critics of Mexico's development argue that the same socioeconomic conditions and political arrangements that characterized the Porfiriato prevail in Mexico today. Many of the country's most important political leaders and private entrepreneurs are descendants of the Porfirian ruling class; wealth is just as concentrated (or more so); high-quality education, health care, and piped water and paved streets are still luxuries unavailable to the poorest sectors of the population; political advancement is denied to individuals and groups who refuse to be co-opted and play by the traditional rules; the press is muzzled; corruption in government security forces is rampant; the influence of foreign capitalists in Mexico's economy is pervasive;

---

[8]Nora Hamilton, *The Limits of State Autonomy: Post-Revolutionary Mexico* (Princeton, N.J.: Princeton University Press, 1982), 281. His government's large investments in public works (electricity, roads, irrigation projects) and its reorganization of the country's financial system laid the foundations for the post-1940 "Mexican miracle" of rapid industrialization and low inflation within a capitalist framework. In the long term, the principal beneficiaries of Cárdenas's economic project proved to be the middle classes and unionized industrial workers—not peasants and the unorganized urban poor.

and the government still resorts to repression to eliminate dissident political and labor leaders.

Much in Mexico's recent experience supports this view of continuity between prerevolutionary and postrevolutionary regimes, but some important differences are noticeable. Individual mobility within Mexico's national political elite is greater than in the Porfirian dictatorship, even if many of those in power today do come from families that were economically or politically prominent in that era. Police corruption is still endemic, but it is now a major public issue and Mexico's current rulers try to bolster their political position by attacking it. In today's Mexico, there is more personal freedom; government repression of opposition groups is less overt, more selective, and less violent (opponents are more likely to be bought off than jailed or killed); opposition parties are tolerated and can campaign openly; there is harsh criticism of government officials and government performance in some quarters of the print media; wealth and social well-being are still distributed very unevenly among the population, but the sources of today's wealth are more diverse. Mexico is now a predominantly urban, semi-industrialized country, in which the majority of the economically active population is employed in the service sector. In agriculture, the traditional rural aristocracy is now overshadowed by agribusiness—huge corporate farms, both domestic and foreign-owned. The government, as owner of Mexico's oil and gas industry, no longer depends on taxation of private enterprise for the bulk of its revenues.

Mexico's political culture and political institutions were also altered by the turmoil of 1910 to 1940, which continues to influence attitudes toward the country's political system. A residue of the widespread violence of that period, which killed one of every seven Mexicans, is a general fear of civil disorder and uncontrolled mass mobilization. The prospect of another wholesale disintegration of the social and political order is viewed with alarm not just by Mexico's elites but also by a majority of the poor. Their personal economic risks in a period of protracted political violence would be much greater than those of the elite.

An even more important political legacy of the 1910 to 1940 period was the symbolic capital that accrued from events and public policies pursued during those years: the Revolution itself; the radically worded Constitution of 1917; the labor and agrarian reforms of the Cárdenas administration; and Cárdenas's expropriation of foreign oil companies in 1938. The present Mexican government and the ruling PRI have succeeded in portraying themselves as the true heirs of those who made the Revolution and consolidated its gains: Emiliano Zapata, the framers of the 1917 Constitution, Lázaro Cárdenas, and the rest. As the bearer of that revolutionary tradition, and also because of the prominent role played by peasants and urban workers in the struggles from 1910 to 1940, the regime has been able to depict itself as a populist one, aligned with the interests of the masses. Even today, it is difficult for opposition parties ideologically to the left of the "official" party to devise electoral platforms that effectively distinguish what they advocate from what the PRI and the government claim to stand for, in rhetoric if not in reality.

In this and many other ways, the Mexican political system has been living off the symbolic capital generated during the 1910 to 1940 period, and especially during the Cárdenas administration. During that period, government bureaucrats, public school teachers, and many others acting as agents of the state did make sincere efforts to deal with the problems of workers and peasants. Their activities enticed many low-income Mexicans into the ranks of official party supporters, or at least made them impervious for nearly half a century to the appeals of opposition parties. But it is also true that the regime's symbolic capital has been severely depleted since 1968 and especially during the economic crisis of the 1980s.

The original Cardenista project—emphasizing redistribution of income, full employment, and state patronage for the weaker sectors of Mexican society—still has great influence among the Mexican people—even those born decades after Cárdenas's presidency. It was precisely the public's identification of *Cuauhtémoc* Cárdenas with his father's social reformism—together with anger over recent economic problems—that turned *"neo-Cardenismo"* into such a powerful political force in 1988.

Finally, the Cárdenas era left an institutional legacy: the presidency became the primary institution of Mexico's political structure, with sweeping powers exercised during a constitutionally limited six-year term with no possibility of reelection; the military was removed from overt political competition and transformed into one of several institutional pillars of the regime; and an elaborate network of government-sponsored peasant and labor organizations provided a mass base for the official political party and performed a variety of political and economic control functions, utilizing a multilayered system of patronage and clientelism.

By 1940 a much larger proportion of the Mexican population was nominally included in the national political system, mostly by their membership in peasant and labor organizations created under Cárdenas. No real democratization of the system resulted from this vast expansion of "political participation," however. Although working-class groups did have more control over their representatives in the government-sponsored organizations than over their former masters on the haciendas and in the factories, their influence over public policy and government priorities after Cárdenas was minimal and highly indirect. Policy recommendations, official actions, and nominations for elective and appointive positions at all levels still emanated from the central government and official party headquarters in Mexico City, filtering down the hierarchy to the rank and file for ratification and legitimation. Cárdenas's experiment with democratization was centered in the workplace.[9]

---

[9]Alicia Hernández, *Cardenismo and the Mexican Political System* (Berkeley: University of California Press, forthcoming 1992). Workers would participate in economic decision making in their ejido or industrial plant. The outcome was greater "workplace democracy" during Cárdenas's presidency, but hardly the "workers' democracy" that in 1938 he claimed would be the end result of his political institution building.

International Environment

Since independence, Mexico's politics and public policies have always been influenced to some extent by proximity to the United States. Porfirio Díaz is widely reputed to have exclaimed, "Poor Mexico! So far from God and so close to the United States." Indeed, this proximity has made the United States a powerful presence in Mexico. The 2,000-mile land border between the two countries, Mexico's rich supplies of minerals, labor, and other resources needed by U.S. industry, and Mexico's attractiveness as a site for U.S. private investment made such influence inevitable.

Midway through the nineteenth century, Mexico's sovereignty as a nation was directly threatened when the United States' push for territorial and economic expansion met little resistance in northern Mexico. Emerging from a war for independence from Spain and plagued by chronic political instability, Mexico was highly vulnerable to aggression from the north. By annexing Texas in 1845 and instigating the Mexican-American War of 1846-48 (Ulysses S. Grant later called it "America's great unjust war"), the United States was able to seize half of Mexico's national territory: disputed land in Texas, all the land that is now California, Nevada, and Utah, most of New Mexico and Arizona, and part of Colorado and Wyoming. This massive seizure of territory, along with several later military interventions and meddling in the politics of "revolutionary" Mexico that extended through the 1920s, left scars that have not healed. Even today, the average Mexican suspects that the United States has designs upon Mexico's remaining territory, its oil, even its human resources.

The lost territory includes the U.S. regions that have been the principal recipients of Mexican immigrant workers in this century. This labor migration, too, was instigated mainly by the United States. Beginning in the 1880s, U.S. farmers, railroads, and mining companies, with U.S. government encouragement, obtained many of the workers needed to expand the economy and transport systems of the Southwest and Midwest by sending labor recruiters into northern and central Mexico.

By the end of the 1920s, the economies of Mexico and the United States were sufficiently intertwined that the effects of the Great Depression were swiftly transmitted to Mexico, causing employment, export earnings, and GNP to plummet. In response to these economic shocks, Mexico tried during the 1930s to reduce its dependence on the United States as a market for silver and other exports. The effort failed, and by 1940 Mexico was more dependent than before on the flow of goods, capital, and labor to and from the United States. Even during the economically nationalist Cárdenas administration, Mexican officials were not really in control of the Mexican economy; too much depended upon external economic conditions, foreign trade flows, and the policies of the U.S. Treasury and other agencies.

After 1940, Mexico relied even more heavily upon U.S. private capital to help finance its drive for industrialization. It was also during the 1940s, when the United States experienced severe shortages of labor in World War II, that Mexico's dependence upon the United States as a market for its surplus labor became institutionalized through the so-called bracero program of importing contract labor. Operating from 1942 to 1964, this program brought more than four million Mexicans to the United States to work in seasonal agriculture.

The United States' stake in Mexico's continued political stability and economic development has increased dramatically since World War II. Mexico is now the third largest trading partner of the United States (behind Canada and Japan), with the two-way trade between them exceeding $60 billion annually. Employment for hundreds of thousands of people in both Mexico and the United States depends on this trade. In 1982, when U.S. trade with Mexico fell by 32 percent because of Mexico's economic crisis, an estimated 250,000 jobs were lost in the United States.

Mexico has also become one of the preferred sites for investments by United States-based multinational corporations, especially for investments in modern industries like petrochemicals, pharmaceuticals, food processing, machinery, and transportation. Subsidiaries of U.S. companies produce half the manufactured goods exported by Mexico. Foreign capital has also been actively sought by firms in Mexico's own private sector, for new joint ventures and to expand plant facilities.

Beyond the more than $18 billion that U.S. firms have directly invested in Mexico, U.S. commercial banks have loaned huge sums to both the Mexican government and private companies in

Mexico. By the end of 1988, Mexico had foreign debts of more than $100 billion, of which $70 billion came from 600 commercial banks. Most of this money flooded into Mexico during the oil boom years of 1978 to 1981, when the largest U.S. banks vigorously competed against one another to make loans to Mexico, whose vast oil collateral seemed to guarantee high profits and low risks to the lenders. Rising interest rates on those loans, a result of the U.S. Federal Reserve Board's tight-money policies designed to combat inflation in the U.S. economy, were a major factor in the Mexican financial crisis that erupted in 1982. After 1982 the flow of funds changed direction, with Mexico becoming a net exporter of capital to the United States. This change was due both to huge interest payments on the debt owed to U.S. banks and to the deposit of an estimated $50 billion in U.S. banks by Mexican nationals seeking a safe haven for their assets.

In the late 1970s, to reduce dependence on the United States, Mexican policymakers embarked on a strategy of diversifying their country's international economic relations. A rapid increase in oil exports was to be the key instrument for achieving this goal. Mexico pushed hard to sell more oil to Japan and Western Europe and succeeded in reducing the U.S. share of its oil exports from 80 percent in the 1975-80 period to 50 percent in 1981-87.[10] Nevertheless, Mexico's overall dependence on the United States—for capital investment, export markets, technology, tourism, and employment opportunities—continues to increase.

The Mexican government's principal strategy for recovering from the economic crisis of the 1980s was to stimulate the production of manufactured goods for export, mainly to the United States. This policy has been remarkably successful, with Mexico's non-oil exports rising from 21 percent of the total in 1982 to 65 percent in 1989. But reliance on the U.S. market for consumer electronics, auto parts, and other key manufactured exports leaves Mexico highly vulnerable to cyclical economic downturns in the United States. That country buys nearly 70 percent of Mexico's exports, and for each percentage decline in the U.S. gross domestic product, Mexico's exports fall by 2.5 percent.

Mexico's external economic dependence has often been cited by both critics and defenders of the Mexican system as an all-encompassing explanation for the country's problems. In fact, economic ties between Mexico and the United States usually explain only part of the picture. And these linkages do not necessarily

---

[10]Gabriel Székely, "Dilemmas of Export Diversification in a Developing Economy: Mexican Oil in the 1980s," *World Development* 17:11 (1989): 1777-97.

predetermine the choices of policy and developmental priorities that are set by Mexico's rulers. But Mexico's economic relationships with the United States and with the international economy do limit the kinds and scope of changes that might be effected in Mexico's political system and development model; and international economic fluctuations have become the largest source of uncertainty in Mexico's planning and policy making.

The crucial role played by foreign capital in Mexico's overall strategy of capitalist development makes it imperative for the Mexican state to maintain a favorable investment climate. Traditionally it has done so by imposing discipline and wage restraint on Mexico's labor force (through government-controlled labor unions), providing generous fiscal incentives and infrastructure for investors (both foreign and domestic), keeping taxes low, and maintaining political stability.

More recently, foreign capital has been courted by liberalizing regulations for such investment (allowing up to 100 percent foreign ownership of many new firms, versus the traditional limit of 49 percent) and opening up more sectors of the economy to foreign investment—sectors formerly reserved for domestic investors or the government itself. Beginning in 1990, the Mexican government added to these incentives by proposing a U.S.-Mexico-Canada free trade agreement, which would make Mexico a more attractive investment site for U.S. firms seeking low-cost labor. While President Salinas opposed such an agreement during his electoral campaign, because "there is such a different economic level between the U.S. and Mexico,"[11] he soon found himself with no alternative to pursuing greater economic integration with the United States. With one million new job seekers entering its labor force each year, Mexico desperately needs to increase its rate of economic growth, and the only way to do that while containing inflation is to stimulate a massive new infusion of investment capital from abroad.

As the U.S. and Mexican economies have become more closely linked, scrutiny of Mexico's political process by U.S. officials and the U.S. media has increased. The fiscal mismanagement symbolized by Mexico's economic crisis of the 1980s eroded U.S. confidence in the Mexican government and raised concern about its ability to maintain political stability. Simultaneously, the United States' heightened preoccupation with illicit drugs—most of which now reach the United States via Mexico—has led members of the U.S. Congress and other officials to publicly criticize police and government corruption in Mexico, which is viewed as a sig-

---

[11]*New York Times*, March 28, 1990.

nificant facilitator of the drug traffic. Finally, as Mexican opposition parties increasingly turned to the U.S. media, the U.S. Congress, and international human rights organizations to voice complaints about electoral fraud by the PRI-government apparatus, the halting and incomplete character of Mexico's democratization has become an issue in U.S.-Mexican relations. International observation of elections has become common in Latin America in recent years, and all significant Mexican opposition parties and even some elements of the PRI have endorsed such scrutiny; but the Mexican government rejects international observers as an unacceptable dilution of national sovereignty. The transition to a more competitive political system in Mexico will make bilateral tensions over such issues increasingly unavoidable in the future.

Political Structure and Institutions

MEXICO'S REGIME TYPE

Mexico's political system has long defied easy classification. In the 1950s and '60s some U.S. political scientists depicted the regime as a "one-party democracy" that was evolving toward "true" (North Atlantic-style) democracy. Certain imperfections were recognized; but in the view of these analysts, political development in Mexico was simply incomplete. After the government massacre of student protesters in 1968, most analysts began describing the system as "authoritarian," but even this characterization was subject to qualification. Mexico now seems to belong to that rapidly expanding category of hybrid, part-free, part-authoritarian systems that do not conform to classical typologies.[12] Such labels as "selective democracy," "hard-line democracy," "*democradura*" (a Spanish contraction of "democracy" and "dictatorship"), and "modernizing authoritarian regime" have been applied to such systems.[13]

They are characterized by competitive (though not necessarily fair and honest) elections that install governments more committed to maintaining political stability and labor discipline than to expanding democratic freedoms, protecting human rights, or mediating class conflicts. Some regimes of this type are more likely to

---

[12]See Lucian W. Pye, "Political Science and the Crisis of Authoritarianism," *American Political Science Review* 84:1 (March 1990): 3-19.

[13]Guillermo O'Donnell, Philippe C. Schmitter, and Laurence Whitehead, eds., *Transitions from Authoritarian Rule* (Baltimore, Md.: Johns Hopkins University Press, 1986); Catherine M. Conaghan and Rosario Espinal, "Unlikely Transitions to Uncertain Regimes?—Democracy without Compromise in the Dominican Republic and Ecuador," *Journal of Latin American Studies* 22:3 (October 1990): 553-74; Peter H. Smith, "Crisis and Democracy in Latin America," *World Politics*, 43:4 (July 1991): 608-34.

PRI structure

countenance undemocratic practices and procedures (e.g., electoral fraud, selective repression of dissidents) than others.

For most of the period since 1940, Mexico has had a pragmatic and moderate authoritarian regime, not the zealously repressive kind that emerged in Latin America's southern cone in the 1960s and '70s. It has been an institutional system, not a personalistic instrument, which has dealt successfully with one of the most difficult problems for nondemocratic systems: elite renewal and executive succession. The Mexican system has been inclusionary, given to co-optation and incorporation rather than exclusion or elimination of troublesome political forces. It strives to incorporate the broadest possible range of social, economic, and political interests within the official party, its affiliated "mass" organizations, and opposition groups whose activities are sanctioned by the regime. As potentially dissident groups have appeared, their leaders usually have been co-opted into government-controlled organizations, or new organizations have been established under government auspices as vehicles for emerging interests. However, when confronted with unco-optable opposition groups or movements (e.g., students in 1968; the "neo-Cardenistas" since 1987), the regime has responded punitively.

The Mexican state represents a coalition of interests, some within the regime itself, some outside. The state has retained a significant degree of autonomy from elite interests in the civil society. It is not the captive of any particular social segment, even though some groups (e.g., the urban middle classes, organized labor, entrepreneurs) clearly have greater influence and more representatives within the ruling political elite than others. Mexico has a strong state, but not so strong that it can rule in open defiance of the rest of society (as, for example, the Chilean military regime did from 1973 to 1989). Large, national-level opposition parties, movements, and labor unions that are truly beyond government control have not been sanctioned or accepted by the ruling elite; but the state is not able to manipulate all opposition groups all the time, and the strongest of them at least can try to bargain with the government.

On paper, the Mexican government appears to be structured much like the U.S. government: a presidential system, three autonomous branches of government (executive, legislative, judicial) and checks and balances, and federalism with considerable autonomy at the local (municipal) level. In practice, however, Mexico's system of government is far removed from the U.S. model. Decision making is highly centralized. The president, operating with relatively few restraints on his authority, completely dominates the legislative and judicial branches.[14] Both houses of the federal legislature have been dominated continuously by representatives affiliated with the ruling PRI. Opposition party members, who now comprise a significant portion of the lower house of Congress (240 out of 500 seats in the 1988-91 period), can criticize the government and its policies vociferously; but their objections to proposals initiated by the president and backed by his party rarely affect the final shape of legislation. Courts and legislatures at the state level normally mirror the preferences of the state governors, who themselves are handpicked by the incumbent president. The sole exception to this pattern occurred in 1989 in the state of Baja California Norte, where the candidate of the opposition National Action Party was elected governor and the same party also gained control of the state legislature.

At all levels of the system, the overwhelming majority of those who are elected to public office are, in effect, appointed to their positions by higher-ups within the PRI-government apparatus. Until recently, selection as the candidate of the official party has been tantamount to election, except in some municipalities and a handful of congressional districts where opposition parties are so strong that they cannot be ignored. Those elected on the PRI ticket are accountable and responsive not primarily to the people who elected them but to their political patrons within the regime. Most citizens who bother to vote do so with little or no expectation that their votes will influence the outcome of the election. The winner, they recognize, has been predetermined by the selection process within the PRI, which until recently has had little grassroots input. Instead, nominating conventions attended only by party activists have ratified the choices made secretively by officials at higher levels.

These and other features of the Mexican system are common to authoritarian regimes elsewhere: limited (not responsible) pluralism; low popular mobilization, with most citizen participation in the electoral process mobilized by the government itself; competition for public office and government benefits restricted mainly to those who support the system; centralized, often arbitrary decision making by one leader or small group; weak ideological constraints on public policy making; extensive government

---

[14]A particularly striking example of executive domination of the legislature occurred in 1990, when the majority bloc of PRI congressmen voted almost unanimously to reprivatize the country's banking system, which the PRI majority had voted to nationalize in 1982. On both occasions, the Congress was ratifying decisions already taken by the incumbent president.

manipulation of the mass media. As described above, however, the Mexican system is more complex than most of the authoritarian regimes that have ruled other Third World nations in recent decades.

POLITICAL CENTRALISM

Despite the federalist structure of government that is enshrined in the Mexican Constitution and legal codes, with their emphasis on the *municipio libre* (the concept of the "free municipality," able to control its own affairs), Mexico has a highly centralized political system. Since the 1920s, the concentration of decision-making power at the federal level has been continuous. The resulting system of centralized control is generally considered to be one of the main factors underlying Mexico's long-term political stability.[15]

Mexico is divided into thirty-two states and federal territories, and each state is divided into *municipios*—politico-administrative units roughly equivalent in size and governmental functions to county governments in the United States. The municipio is governed by an *ayuntamiento*, or council, headed by a *presidente municipal*. Municipal officials are elected every three years. In practice, each presidente municipal has been handpicked by higher-ups within the PRI-government apparatus, normally a federal congressman (*diputado*) and the state governor.

The absence of popular input into this candidate selection process has often led to the designation of municipal presidents who were intensely disliked by their constituents, and who embarrassed the PRI and the government by their inept handling of local problems. Such outcomes periodically provoke calls for open primary elections within the PRI, to compel the party's candidates to develop a popular support base. An abortive experiment with open primaries was conducted in the mid-1960s, but the idea was resisted adamantly by old-guard PRI leaders, and it was soon dropped. Carlos Madrazo, the PRI national chairman who instigated the reform, was removed from his position.

Another attempt to introduce a system of PRI primary elections at the municipio level was made in the mid-1980s by President Miguel de la Madrid. Implemented in just a few states, the system had mixed results. It worked adequately in some small municipios but not in large cities, where PRI leaders feared that

---

[15]See Richard R. Fagen and William S. Tuohy, *Politics and Privilege in a Mexican City* (Stanford, Calif: Stanford University Press, 1972), 18-41.

open primaries would be divisive and cost the party electoral support. In 1989 President Salinas began authorizing municipal and gubernatorial primaries in certain states where the PRI faced tough competition. At the PRI's fourteenth general assembly held in September 1990, Salinas pushed through a set of changes designed to "democratize" the party's candidate selection process throughout the country. Henceforth, aspiring candidates for municipal offices, congressional seats, and state governorships must demonstrate that they have the support of a specific percentage of the "directive committees" of PRI-affiliated organizations (25-30 percent, depending on the office) or of the registered voters in a given district (10-20 percent). The final selection of PRI candidates will be made at party conventions, to which delegates will be "elected democratically." It remains to be seen whether the new rules will, in fact, make elective positions accessible to all PRI members and reduce the incidence of candidate impositions from above.

These changes represent, at least in part, a response by the ruling elite to the public's growing resentment of centralism and to the resurgence of political regionalism during the 1980s. Regional particularism has been a constant in Mexican politics since the mid-nineteenth century, but it has been especially potent during periods in which the central government is perceived as being less efficacious and legitimate.[16] The economic crisis that erupted in 1982 again focused provincial resentment on the capital and the highly centralized decision-making process, which were blamed for the economic debacle. The crisis also brought a sharp disparity in economic performance between the central core region and other parts of the country. The Mexico City metropolitan area soon became the most depressed region of the country, while other states and regions (e.g., the northern border states; Guadalajara and its hinterland) recovered more quickly from the initial shock and showed considerable economic dynamism in the second half of the decade. This reinforced the belief, widespread in the provinces, that Mexico's problems are centered in the capital.

Regional pride, combined with the increasing rejection by businessmen and the general public of control by a failing central government, became a major source of opposition party strength in municipal and gubernatorial elections held between 1983 and

---

[16]See Paul W. Drake, "Mexican Regionalism Reconsidered," *Journal of Inter-American Affairs* 12:3 (July 1970): 411-20; and Edward J. Williams, "The Resurgent North and Contemporary Mexican Regionalism," *Mexican Studies* 6:2 (Summer 1990): 299-323.

1989 in the northern states. In 1983, the PAN swept to victory in all major cities of Chihuahua, containing more than 70 percent of the state's population. In the state of Baja California Norte in 1989, the vote for the PAN's gubernatorial candidate, Ernesto Ruffo, was so overwhelming that his victory was recognized by the federal government. This marked the first state governorship to be surrendered to an opposition candidate since the official party was founded in 1929.

The Mexico City-based political elite has not been oblivious to these trends. In his 1987-88 presidential campaign, Carlos Salinas ran as the favorite son of the state of Nuevo León, the northern border state where his ancestors settled in the seventeenth century and his parents maintain a home, rather than the Federal District (Mexico City), where he was born and raised. The federal government has been emphasizing economic policies—e.g., deregulation, privatization, stimulation of *maquiladoras* (in-bond assembly plants) and other export-oriented industries—from which many entrepreneurs in the provinces have benefited and with which they are philosophically in tune. Some steps have been taken to rein in the federal security apparatus, especially the hated and feared federal judicial police, which traditionally has been run from Mexico City without regard for the sensibilities of state and local authorities. The Salinas government has taken a cooperative, nonconfrontational stance toward the Panista government of Baja California Norte, hoping to demonstrate that Mexico City could work constructively with at least some kinds of opposition governments in the periphery.

Nevertheless, the consequences of political centralism remain dramatically evident in Mexico today. Each successive layer of government is substantially weaker, less autonomous, and more impoverished than the levels above it. Historically the federal government has controlled about 85 percent of public revenues, the state governments less than 12 percent, and the municipios scarcely 3 percent. The municipios' share has risen to about 5-7 percent of total public spending in recent years. The average municipal government depends on the federal and state governments for about 80 percent of its income; only 20 percent comes from local sources.

Centralism has contributed to extreme inequalities in distribution of public investments and access to public services in Mexico. By the mid-1980s the central region including Mexico City, with about one-third of the country's total population, accounted for nearly half of total federal government expenditures. Thus the average low-income family living in a Mexico City slum is more likely to have access to a basic public service like piped water or sewerage than a family in similar circumstances in a provincial city or a small rural community.

Another manifestation of political centralism in Mexico is the growing predominance within the country's ruling elite of people born or raised in Mexico City. In the López Portillo administration (1976-82), 40 percent of the top officials had been born in Mexico City, compared with only 20 percent among the upper elite holding office during the years 1946-71.[17] The proportion of cabinet members born in Mexico City has increased steadily since the 1940s; by 1990, *capitalinos* held nearly 60 percent of the cabinet posts (see figure 1). Politically ambitious individuals must gravitate to the center of the system or, preferably, be born there. This has been the case with Mexico's five most recent presidents, all of whom were either born or raised in Mexico City.

All five of these presidents entered office pledging to renew the "struggle against centralism," but serious efforts to decentralize have been made only since 1984. Under de la Madrid and Salinas, state and municipal authorities have been involved more fully in the planning of federal development programs affecting their jurisdictions; a limited form of revenue sharing has been implemented and the federal Constitution amended to enhance the capacity of local governments to raise their own revenues; partially successful efforts have been made to shift decision-making authority over public education and health care from the federal government to the states.[18] Nevertheless, the country's 2,378 municipios are still overwhelmingly dependent on the state and federal governments for the funds needed to finance essential public services. State governors retain control over resources transferred from the federal government. Effective administrative decentralization down to the municipio level would require state governors to relinquish a major portion of their political power—something that they have successfully resisted.

THE PRESIDENCY

Mexico's political system is commonly described as a "presidentialist" or "presidentially centered" system. The Mexican presi-

---

[17]Peter H. Smith, *Labyrinths of Power: Political Recruitment in Twentieth-Century Mexico* (Princeton, N.J.: Princeton University Press, 1979): 306.

[18]See John J. Bailey, *Governing Mexico: The Statecraft of Crisis Management* (New York: St. Martin's Press, 1988), 83-86; and Victoria Rodríguez, "The Politics of Decentralization in Mexico, 1970-1986" (Ph.D. dissertation, University of California-Berkeley, 1987).

Figure 1

Representation of Mexico City in Cabinet

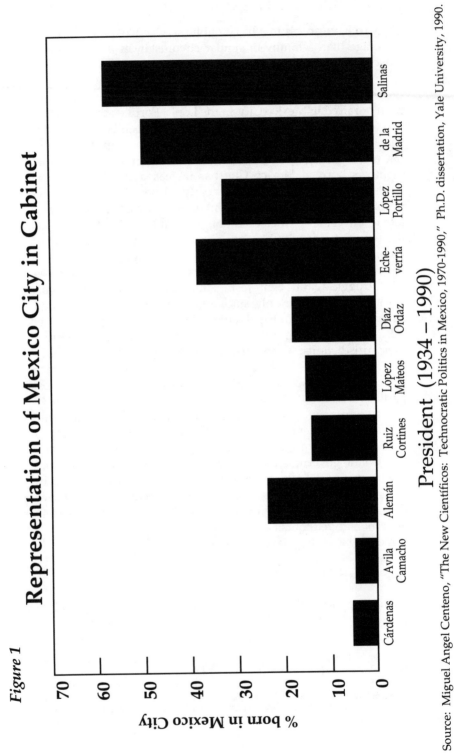

Source: Miguel Angel Centeno, "The New Científicos: Technocratic Politics in Mexico, 1970-1990," Ph.D. dissertation, Yale University, 1990.

dent possesses a broad range of both constitutionally mandated and unwritten, informally recognized powers that assure his dominance over all of the country's other political institutions.[19]

The principle of executive control over the legislative and judicial branches has long been established in the Mexican system. Ratification of the president's policy choices by both houses of the federal Congress has been virtually automatic since the 1930s. The president has introduced most of the legislation considered by the Congress and, in his role as "supreme head" of the official party, secured its enactment. However, with the emergence of a strong opposition presence in Congress as a result of the 1988 elections, the president no longer commands the two-thirds majority required to pass constitutional amendments. Since the 1920s every Mexican president has used amendment of the Constitution as a key instrument for implementing his administration's policy agenda and expanding the prerogatives of the presidency (the 1917 Constitution has been amended more than three hundred times). To revise the Constitution now, the president must build coalitions with one or more opposition parties. In the first two years of his term, President Salinas obtained from the PAN the additional votes necessary for approval of two key constitutional amendments.

The Mexican federal judiciary remains firmly under the control of the president. On any issue that has national political significance, the federal judiciary can be expected to take its cue from the incumbent president. Presidential decrees or legislation enacted at the behest of the president are never found to be unconstitutional by the Mexican Supreme Court, and the Congress rubber-stamps presidential appointments to or dismissals from the federal judiciary.

The absence of a rigid, fully elaborated political ideology makes it possible for a Mexican president to have a pragmatic, flexible program and style of governance. The so-called ideology of the Mexican Revolution is little more than a loosely connected set of goals or symbols: social justice (including agrarian reform), economic nationalism, restricting the influence of the church in public life, and freedom from self-perpetuating, dictatorial rule in the Porfirio Díaz style. There are a few tenets of "revolutionary"

---

[19]For a detailed discussion of the "metaconstitutional" powers of the Mexican president, see Luis Javier Garrido, "The Crisis of *Presidencialismo*," in *Mexico's Alternative Political Futures*, ed. Wayne A. Cornelius, Judith Gentleman, and Peter H. Smith, Monograph Series, no. 30 (La Jolla, Calif.: Center for U.S.-Mexican Studies, University of California, San Diego, 1989), 417-34.

ideology that must still be scrupulously observed, such as the constitutionally mandated no-reelection principle: no official, at any level of the system, can be reelected to the same public office, at least for consecutive terms; the president himself is limited to a single six-year term. But virtually all other elements of revolutionary ideology have been shaded or ignored, at one time or another, by the presidents holding office since 1940. President José López Portillo, for example, declared in 1977 that Mexico's land redistribution program was, for all practical purposes, at an end, because allegedly there was no more land left to distribute to landless peasants. Under Presidents de la Madrid and Salinas, the definition of economic nationalism has shifted from keeping U.S. interests at bay to achieving competitiveness and new markets for Mexico's exports in the world economy, through policies aimed at opening up the Mexican economy to more foreign-made products and foreign direct investment, and linking Mexico's economy even more closely to that of the United States. And Salinas's overtures to the Catholic church show that political pragmatism can take precedence over ideologically grounded state hostility to that key institution of Mexican society.

Neither are Mexican presidents seriously constrained by the mass media. Although the government does not directly censor the media, there can be significant economic penalties for engaging in criticism or investigative reporting that seriously embarrasses the government. Government advertising can be withheld from offending publications. For decades the government could also threaten critical publications with closure by cutting off their supply of newsprint, which could be purchased only from a state-owned company, PIPSA. However, in a concession to advocates of political liberalization, President Salinas eliminated PIPSA's monopoly, allowing publications to buy newsprint directly from foreign manufacturers. Recent presidents have also silenced criticism from some newspapers through government-orchestrated, hostile takeovers of their boards of directors. Finally, cash payments to journalists traditionally have been used to assure favorable treatment of a president and his policies—a practice that has been curtailed somewhat since 1982 as part of a general anticorruption campaign. But except for individual political columnists who often comment vituperatively on the failings of the president and his policies, editorial criticism of an incumbent president remains muted. Whatever they say about a president or his administration, the print media reach only a tiny fraction of the Mexican population (even the largest Mexico City newspapers are believed to have circulations under 100,000), and television is virtually monopolized by a huge private firm, Televisa, which has a notoriously close working relationship with the PRI-government apparatus.[20]

A great part of the Mexican president's power is derived from his ability to select and impose public officeholders at all levels of the system, including his own successor as president. All but a handful of public officeholders in Mexico serve at the pleasure of the president. State governors (except those belonging to an opposition party), the leaders of Congress and the PRI, some high-ranking military officers, the heads of state-owned industrial enterprises, and hundreds of other officeholders are handpicked by each incoming president. Even the leaders of large, government-affiliated labor unions may be removed by the president, as Carlos Salinas demonstrated within several months of taking office by sacking two of Mexico's most powerful and corrupt labor chieftains.[21] Public officials whose actions have proven embarrassing, disruptive, or otherwise troublesome to the president or to his inner circle of advisers can be arbitrarily removed. Even popularly elected state governors who fall badly out of favor with the president are faced with almost instant dismissal, which the president can accomplish in a variety of ways. He can appoint the governor to a lesser, nonelective position or force him into retirement. Should the offending governor resist, the president can have the PRI-controlled federal Senate declare the state government "dissolved." Sometimes a state governor is cashiered for failing to deliver a sufficiently large majority of votes for the PRI in his state; such was the fate of three governors of states carried by opposition candidate Cuauhtémoc Cárdenas in the 1988 presidential election. This absolute power to seat and unseat state governors has been a key element of presidential power in Mexico since the 1920s.

Even though the Mexican president wields great power, he does so within certain limits, perhaps the most important of which are unwritten, de facto constraints generally recognized and accepted within Mexico's political and economic elites. Sometimes

---

[20]Dismissing criticism of Televisa's numbingly one-sided, pro-PRI coverage of the 1988 presidential campaigns, the conglomerate's president publicly declared himself to be a PRIista and explained that "if Televisa does not cover the campaigns of the opposition politicians, it is because they are not saying anything new" (*Latin America Weekly Report*, February 11, 1988, 8).

[21]They were the long-time leader of the petroleum workers' union, Joaquín Hernández Galicia, alias "La Quina," who was forcibly removed from his house by army troops and imprisoned for illegal stockpiling of firearms; and Carlos Jonguitud Barrios, leader "for life" of the national teachers' union (Mexico's largest labor union), who "resigned after a private meeting with President Salinas," according to an official account (Presidencia de México, *Mexican Agenda: Background Information on Mexico*, April 1990, 7).

these constraints have limited presidential autonomy in key policy areas. For example, President Luis Echeverría often blamed his economic policy failures on the machinations of the business elite centered in the city of Monterrey, and there is evidence that in 1972 big business forced Echeverría to drop his plan to increase the tax burden on the wealthy.[22] When some presidents went ahead and broke the established rules of the game in conspicuous ways—for example, by shooting the children of urban middle-class parents in the Tlatelolco massacre (Gustavo Díaz Ordaz in 1968); by expropriating large, prosperous landholdings in the state of Sonora (Luis Echeverría in 1976); and by running up the country's external debt irresponsibly and nationalizing the banks (José López Portillo, 1977-82)—the moral and political authority of the presidency began to erode and private-sector confidence in the government was shaken. Miguel de la Madrid's failure to provide effective leadership after the devastating Mexico City earthquakes of September 1985 and his inability to engineer a sustained recovery from the economic crisis that he inherited from his predecessor further reinforced the image of a weakened, ineffectual, and "devalued" presidency.[23] De la Madrid became the first Mexican president to be heckled and jeered by opposition congressmen during his annual state-of-the-nation address—a practice that has continued in the Salinas presidency.

By the end of de la Madrid's term, the conventional wisdom held that traditional Mexican *presidencialismo*—especially when defined as the ability of the president to take unilateral actions that may be damaging to the interests of key political and economic elites—was dead, the victim of the excesses of Díaz Ordaz, Echeverría, and López Portillo and the leadership failures of de la Madrid. Upon taking office in 1988, Carlos Salinas challenged this notion through a succession of bold strokes against the fiefdoms that had progressively challenged presidential prerogatives during the preceding four administrations (e.g., the oil workers' union) and by embracing new policies that entailed large political

---

[22]See Samuel S. Schmidt, *El deterioro del presidencialismo mexicano: Los años de Luis Echeverría* (México, D.F.: EDAMEX, 1986); and Leopoldo Solís, *Economic Policy Reform in Mexico: A Case Study for Developing Countries* (New York: Pergamon, 1981), 73-76. On the Monterrey business elite and its often contentious relationship with the central government, see Alex M. Saragoza, *The Monterrey Elite and the Mexican State, 1880-1940* (Austin: University of Texas Press, 1988).

[23]The term "devalued" was used in late 1982 by José López Portillo to characterize his own presidency, which ended amid Mexico's gravest economic crisis since the Great Depression.

risks (e.g., a free trade agreement with the United States). These actions proved that the essential powers of Mexican presidencialismo were still intact and could be used to effect sweeping political and economic change.

Nevertheless, several developments are likely to reduce the power of the Mexican presidency in the long run. The shift since 1982 away from a statist model of development and toward market-oriented economic policies could have such an effect. Privatizing state-owned enterprises and dismantling government controls over large parts of the economy will inevitably reduce the state's role as "rector" (guide) of the economy and the president's power to influence the path of national development. Presidential prerogatives may also be eroded by steps toward political modernization. For example, Salinas's strategy to rejuvenate the PRI depends heavily on giving more autonomy to local party officials and committees in such matters as the selection of PRI candidates. This implies that the president must now negotiate with lower-echelon party leaders rather than simply impose his own choices. If Salinas or his successors succeed in modernizing the PRI, they may lay the groundwork for a very different kind of presidencialismo—one that will have to rely more on skillful negotiation and alliance building with actors throughout the political system.

Some analysts see the presidency itself as the foremost obstacle to political liberalization.[24] According to this view, any changes (e.g., "allowing" opposition parties to win state governorships) that dilute the direct influence of the president would threaten regime stability, because such changes violate the fundamental logic of a presidentially centered system. This provides a continuing rationale for highly centralized, authoritarian control by the president. No coalition governments—with representatives of the opposition parties in charge of government ministries—or other forms of power sharing with the opposition are possible, as they might be in a parliamentary system. Thus, Mexico's transition to a more competitive, more democratic political system is likely to be more protracted and painful because of its presidentialist system. The counterargument is that strong presidential leadership will be a necessary—though by no means sufficient—condition of political liberalization, because of the weakness of proreform opposition parties and the strength of antireform elements within the official party and its affiliated organizations.

---

[24]See, for example, Lorenzo Meyer, "Democratization of the PRI: Mission Impossible?" in *Mexico's Alternative Political Futures*, ed. Cornelius, Gentleman, and Smith, 343-44.

It is generally believed that an incumbent president has the power to select his own successor. In September 1990, Luis Echeverría became the first former president to publicly acknowledge this crucially important, unwritten rule of the Mexican system. However, the actual process of selecting a new president remains shrouded in secrecy.[25] The man chosen is popularly referred to as *el tapado* (literally, the "hidden one" or the "hooded one") until his identity is made public (an act known as the *destape*, or "unveiling") by PRI leaders to whom the president has communicated his choice (through the *"dedazo,"* or pointing of the presidential finger).

Some analysts have argued (with no proof) that the outgoing president consults behind the scenes with former presidents, national-level leaders of the government-affiliated labor movement and other PRI sectors, and key representatives of other groups like the military and the business community. The president may or may not choose to respect their views when he makes the final selection.[26] Other analysts contend that these consultations are mainly a means of co-opting the PRI leadership and discouraging dissident factions within the party from launching their own candidates; all that really counts in the selection process is the preference of the incumbent president.

The final choice is probably made through some highly idiosyncratic weighing of factors like personal relationships that the outgoing president has developed with potential successors over his entire career; which of these men is most likely to continue the basic policies of the outgoing president; the actual performance of various members of the presidential cabinet (from whom the new president is likely to be chosen) during the administration now ending; the political and economic groups to which possible successors seem to be allied; and what is known as *la coyuntura*—the conjuncture of economic and political circumstances that Mexico confronts at home and abroad as the moment of presidential succession approaches. These circumstances indicate the kinds of problems that the next president may have to handle. For example,

---

[25]For attempts to codify the informal rules of presidential succession in Mexico, see Smith, *Labyrinths of Power*, chap. 10; Peter H. Smith, "The 1988 Presidential Succession in Historical Perspective," in *Mexico's Alternative Political Futures*, ed. Cornelius, Gentleman, and Smith; and Luis Javier Garrido, "Las quince reglas de la sucesión presidencial," in *La sucesión presidencial en 1988*, ed. Abrahám Nuncio (México, D.F.: Grijalbo, 1988).

[26]See, for example, Frank Brandenburg, *The Making of Modern Mexico* (Englewood Cliffs, N.J.: Prentice-Hall, 1964), 145-50.

the financial crisis that began in 1981 is thought to have boosted the presidential prospects of Miguel de la Madrid, who had established his credentials as an expert on public finance, while diminishing the chances of several other cabinet members who were perceived as traditional politicians. By contrast, it was thought that the worsening of the regime's legitimacy crisis and the emergence of serious divisions within the political elite during de la Madrid's term would give the advantage in 1988 to candidates who had greater experience in political management and negotiation. Instead, de la Madrid turned to his right-hand man of the previous thirteen years, Carlos Salinas de Gortari, the most "technocratic" of the three principal contenders and the one with the least experience in practical politics. De la Madrid's choice of Salinas demonstrated the importance of loyal, effective service to the outgoing president as well as de la Madrid's concern about policy continuity. As the principal architect of the economic stabilization and restructuring program launched in 1983, Salinas was by far the best equipped and most strongly disposed among the leading precandidates to complete the implementation of de la Madrid's most important policy initiative.

By tradition, those who aspire to the presidency of Mexico cannot openly promote their candidacies or even admit that they are seeking the office. Excessively open campaigning can be fatal, as the widely acknowledged front-runner in 1976, Gobernación Secretary Mario Moya Palencia, discovered. (Outgoing President Echeverría chose a dark-horse candidate, Finance Minister José López Portillo, to succeed him.) The supporters of the major contenders work diligently behind the scenes to advance the chances of their man and to discredit the other contenders. In 1987, in response to widespread criticism of the traditional, secretive selection process, Miguel de la Madrid, acting through the president of the PRI, publicly identified six "distinguished party members" as precandidates for the PRI's 1988 presidential nomination and arranged for them to present their ideas to PRI notables at semipublic breakfast meetings. These appearances represented only a cosmetic change in the presidential succession process, however, since they provoked no real debate or public campaigning by the hopefuls, and the outgoing president remained firmly in control of the nomination process. "In accordance with tradition, virtually every member of the official party watched and waited for months for a signal 'from above' before deciding to support one of the six precandidates. When President de la Madrid gave that signal in favor of Carlos Salinas de Gortari, virtually the entire party

jumped on the bandwagon."[27] In the end, de la Madrid's innovation only called attention to the closed, authoritarian nature of the
presidential succession process and the highly circumscribed role
of the PRI in that process, at least as it has operated in recent
decades.[28]

Anticipating even stronger criticism of the traditional system
when the next succession begins, Carlos Salinas in 1990 put into
place a new mechanism for formally designating the PRI's presidential candidate. Rather than being so conspicuously handpicked
by the outgoing president, the PRI's nominee for the 1994-2000
term will have to win a majority of votes within a "national
political council" consisting of 150 senior party officials. This pro-
cedure falls considerably short of an open, participatory selection
process; nor does it force the outgoing president to relinquish
control over the outcome. The selection committee is likely to be
packed with party leaders personally loyal to Salinas, and their
votes will undoubtedly reflect his preference.

However the selection is actually made, it is clear that the
outgoing president chooses from a very short list: a handful of
incumbent cabinet members, which in recent transitions has included the secretaries of Gobernación (responsible for management of elections and internal security), planning and budget,
finance, labor, education, and energy and state industries; and the
mayor of Mexico City, who holds cabinet rank. These men are the
survivors of protracted and intense political and bureaucratic
competition within the regime. In this sense, the power of the
incumbent president to determine who will succeed him is circumscribed by the political system itself and how it operates to
thrust certain kinds of men to the top of the political pyramid.

Precisely because Mexican presidents are so much a product
of the system over which they preside, it is often argued that policy
shifts from one administration to another are likely to be limited.
According to this view, it is not only the incoming president's own
socialization and personal political alliances that constrain him in
formulating new policy directions. He must also respond to the
regime's traditional mass support groups whose cooperation with
his government is needed. The possibilities of truly major shifts in
policy are further diminished by external economic conditions (for
example, a world oil glut) that limit government revenues and

---

[27]Meyer, "Democratization of the PRI," 343.

[28]In the 1940s and 1950s, until the transfer of power from Ruiz Cortines to López
Mateos in 1958, the presidential succession process was marked by considerably
more open competition and debate within the ruling party.

create obstacles to the success of policies that the incoming president might prefer.

Other observers of Mexican politics argue that, though radical policy departures by incoming presidents are improbable within this system, meaningful "readjustments" of policy orientation and political style are both feasible and necessary to maintain political stability. They point to the oscillations that seem to have occurred from one *sexenio* (six-year administration) to another, on a rough kind of left-right, progressive-conservative continuum, since consolidation of the postrevolutionary central government in the 1920s. This is the so-called pendulum theory of Mexican politics (see figure 2).

Some Mexican presidents since 1920 have been more conservative than others in personal convictions as well as public policies: Plutarco Calles (Cárdenas's predecessor), in his later years; Miguel Alemán (1946-52); Díaz Ordaz (1964-70); and de la Madrid (1982-88). Similarly, presidents like Cárdenas, Adolfo López Mateos (1958-64), and Luis Echeverría (1970-76) have pursued some policies and used rhetoric that was more progressive or reformist. Still other presidents (Avila Camacho, 1940-46; Ruiz Cortines, 1946-52; López Portillo, at least during the first three years of his term) are viewed as transitional figures, consolidators of the status quo. The "center" of the Mexican political spectrum is not fixed. It can be moved in one direction or the other by the actions or policies of a president. Cárdenas's expropriation of the foreign oil companies in 1938, López Portillo's nationalization of the banks in 1982, and Salinas's call for a North American free trade zone in 1990 are examples of presidential acts that defined a new political equilibrium. Whatever personal or political considerations may have influenced these decisions, they impressively demonstrated the power of the modern Mexican president to chart a new course.

CAMARILLAS AND CLIENTELISM

An important reason why each incoming president is able to imprint his personal style and at least some of his policy preferences upon the PRI-government apparatus lies in the clientage structures that permeate the Mexican political system. The entire system can be viewed as consisting of interlocking chains of patron-client relationships, in which the "patrons"—persons having higher political status—provide benefits such as protection, support in political struggles with rivals, and chances for upward political or economic mobility to their "clients"—persons having

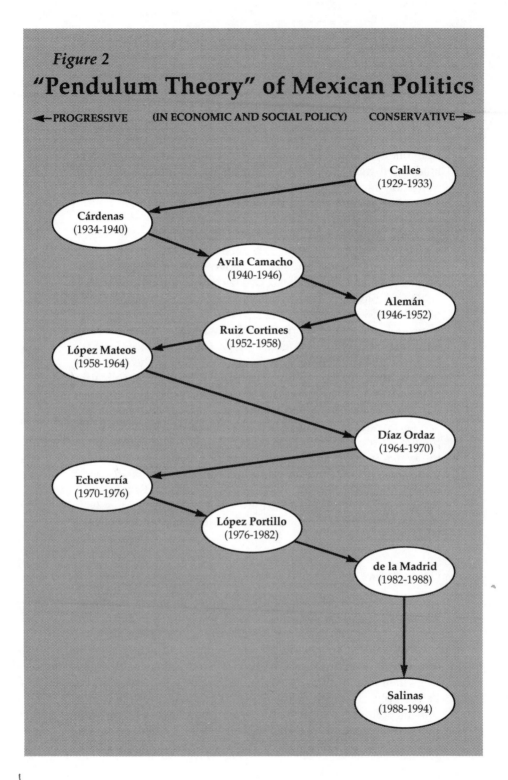

Figure 2

"Pendulum Theory" of Mexican Politics

◄–PROGRESSIVE   (IN ECONOMIC AND SOCIAL POLICY)   CONSERVATIVE–►

Calles
(1929-1933)

Cárdenas
(1934-1940)

Avila Camacho
(1940-1946)

Alemán
(1946-1952)

Ruiz Cortines
(1952-1958)

López Mateos
(1958-1964)

Díaz Ordaz
(1964-1970)

Echeverría
(1970-1976)

López Portillo
(1976-1982)

de la Madrid
(1982-1988)

Salinas
(1988-1994)

lesser political status. In exchange, the "clients" provide loyalty, deference, and useful services like voter mobilization, political control, and problem solving to their patrons within the official party or government bureaucracy.[29]

The chains of patron-client relationships are interwoven, because patrons do not want to limit themselves to one client, and clients avoid pinning all their hopes on a single patron. Normally these interweaving chains of clientage relationships come together at the apex of the national authority structure—the presidency. For all those who hold office during a given sexenio, the president is the supreme patron. The vertical grouping of several different levels of patron-client relationships is popularly known in Mexico as a *camarilla*—roughly translated, a "political clique" (see figure 3). Each camarilla has been assembled over a long period of time, through an elaborate process of personal alliance building. Most of the truly important political conflict and competition in the Mexican system is related in some way to the constant struggle between rival camarillas. Especially at the cabinet level, the camarillas vie constantly for influence over national policy making in key areas. They also struggle for control over strategically situated political offices, such as cabinet ministries. Above all, throughout the sexenio they jockey for position in the race for the presidency itself. The cabinet ministers who lead the rival camarillas are often, themselves, aspirants to the presidency.

Because reelection to the presidency is prohibited, the "supreme patron" in this elaborate clientage structure is replaced every six years. The new president has his own camarilla, whose members, in turn, have different followers of their own, and so on down the system. The government-wide shuffling of officeholders at the beginning of each new presidential administration actually amounts to substituting one major camarilla—the one that will now control the presidency—for another (the one headed by the outgoing president).

The basic element that binds camarillas together is personal loyalty to the camarilla leader rather than ideology. The members of the winning camarilla may, indeed, share certain policy preferences or career experiences that distinguish them from previous administrations, but the essential bond is loyalty to the man who

---

[29]Clientelistic relationships are by no means limited to the political system. For an analysis of the continuing importance of clientelism as a way of structuring interaction and control throughout Mexican society, see Luis Roniger, *Hierarchy and Trust in Modern Mexico and Brazil* (New York: Praeger, 1990).

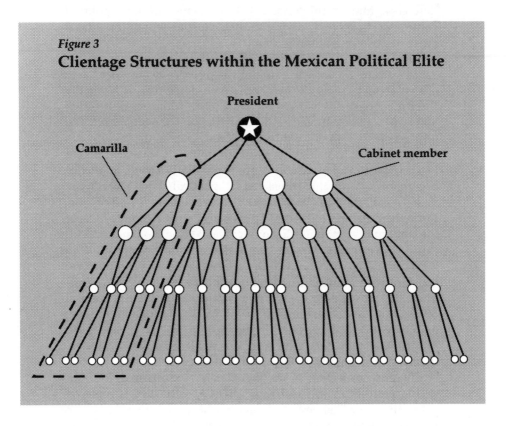

Figure 3

Clientage Structures within the Mexican Political Elite

holds the presidency, from whom all policy and stylistic cues are taken.

One major consequence of this kind of political elite structure is that there is no room for political or policy innovation from below. No rational aspirant to power at lower levels of the system will take the risk of doing things that go beyond the well-recognized rules of the game. Thus, if the political system is to be reformed, it must be done "from the top," as a supreme exertion of presidential will. Another consequence is that the responsiveness and accountability of officials to the PRI's "mass constituencies" and to the general public is greatly diminished. Fervent, unquestioning loyalty and service to one's immediate superior in the PRI-government apparatus is the only promising route to upward political mobility. Even for elected officeholders like members of Congress, the official's only real constituency is his boss—his principal patron within the multilayered clientage structure. It is that person who will determine the officeholder's next position within the system.[30] Empirical analysis has demonstrated that camarilla membership—who one knows and serves—is perhaps the best predictor of survival in the bureaucratic elite.[31]

To move up the hierarchy, a person must be concerned not only about joining the "right" camarilla but with building one's own. The larger and more diverse the camarilla, the more tentacles it extends into all parts of the government bureaucracy and the PRI, the more powerful its leader is. The strongest camarillas built in recent sexenios have also linked several different generations of political leaders. For example, Carlos Salinas's camarilla links him, through family, school, or career ties, to practically every member of the economic cabinet who has held office since the 1940s.[32] When the camarilla leader moves vertically or horizontally within the political system, the key members of his team move with him. For example, Carlos Salinas followed his boss, Miguel de la Madrid, from the Treasury Ministry to the Ministry of Planning and Budget when de la Madrid was promoted to cabinet rank.

Joining the "wrong" camarilla can entail high career costs, but it is not necessarily fatal to one's long-term political prospects. All successful political leaders in Mexico are associated with multiple camarillas at different points in their careers.[33] It is acceptable to shift loyalties when the upward mobility of one's political mentor has been blocked. Politically agile individuals who have built personal alliances with some members of a rival camarilla can often jump directly from a losing camarilla to the winning one. For example, after Mario Moya Palencia lost out to José López Portillo in the 1976 presidential succession, many members of Moya Palen-

---

[30]In the case of Congress, the effects of the camarilla system are reinforced by the prohibition on immediate reelection introduced into the federal Constitution in 1933. Members of the Chamber of Deputies and Senate must skip at least one term before they can run again for a congressional seat. Under this system, it is the president and his agents (senior PRI leaders) who decide where members of Congress will go after their terms expire—not their constituents. See Jeffrey A. Weldon, "No Reelection and the Mexican Congress" (Ph.D. dissertation, University of California, San Diego, in progress).

[31]Miguel Angel Centeno and Jeffrey Weldon, "A Small Circle of Friends: Elite Survival in Mexico" (paper presented at the International Congress of the Latin American Studies Association, Washington, D.C., April 1991).

[32]Centeno and Weldon, "A Small Circle of Friends." See also Roderic A. Camp, "Comparing Political Generations in Mexico: The Last One Hundred Years" (paper presented at the VIII Conference of Mexican and North American Historians, San Diego, October 1990).

[33]See Roderic A. Camp, "Camarillas in Mexican Politics: The Case of the Salinas Cabinet," *Mexican Studies* 6:1 (Winter 1990): 85-107.

cia's very large camarilla were able to gain positions in the López Portillo and de la Madrid administrations. One of them, Carlos Salinas, became president in 1988. Similarly, when Salinas's chief rival for the presidency, Jesús Silva Herzog, was forced to resign his cabinet post in 1986, key members of his camarilla quickly switched to Salinas's team. One of them, Jaime Serra Puche, became Salinas's commerce secretary. Even disappointed presidential contenders sometimes receive cabinet posts in the next administration if they "discipline" themselves sufficiently. Providing jobs for losing camarilla leaders and their followers serves as a balancing and conciliating mechanism for the political system. It helps to ensure stability by providing even the losing factions with an incentive for remaining within the official fold, waiting out the current sexenio and positioning themselves for the next one.

Recruiting the Political Elite

What kinds of people gain entry into Mexico's national political elite, and who makes it to the top? At least since the days of the Porfiriato, the Mexican political elite has been recruited predominantly from the middle class. The 1910 Revolution did not open up the political elite to large numbers of people from peasant or urban laborer backgrounds. That occurred only in the 1930s, during the Cárdenas administration, and then mainly at the local and state levels rather than among the national-level elite. A study of the national bureaucratic elite in power in 1984 found that 93 percent came from the middle to upper classes.[34]

The 1910 Revolution did, however, increase rates of political mobility for the country's middle class, and it redistributed power within that class. Power shifted from those who had become entrenched in the Porfirian dictatorship to the politically dispossessed elements of the middle class: ambitious, well-educated people whose political aspirations had been blocked during the Porfiriato. The Revolution opened up many public offices and created new routes to power for such people. Over the next sixty years, middle-class persons with literary skills (intellectuals, journalists) and those with military experience and backgrounds in electoral politics were gradually supplanted by middle-class people with different skills and professional training: lawyers, engineers, agronomists, planners, and, most recently, economists and professional public administrators—the so-called *técnicos* (technocrats) of recent presidential administrations.[35]

---

[34]Miguel Angel Centeno, "The New Científicos: Technocratic Politics in Mexico, 1970-1990" (Ph.D. dissertation, Yale University, 1990). This analysis is based on a sample of 867 members of the federal government bureaucracy at the level of director-general or above.

[35]See Peter S. Cleaves, *Professions and the State: The Mexican Case* (Tucson: University of Arizona Press, 1987), 87-105.

In recent sexenios, the national political elite has become more homogeneous in several important ways. As pointed out above (see figure 1), its members have been drawn increasingly from the ranks of *capitalinos*—people born or raised in Mexico City. Most receive their undergraduate degrees at the National University in Mexico City (UNAM), which continues to serve as a crucial training and meeting ground for aspirants to political power, despite the increased importance in recent years of elite private institutions of higher learning. Luis Echeverría and José López Portillo were classmates at UNAM. Miguel de la Madrid was López Portillo's student in the UNAM law school. Carlos Salinas took public administration courses from Miguel de la Madrid at UNAM. Part-time teaching at UNAM or other universities is one of the most important ways in which an aspirant to political power can identify and recruit bright new talent for the camarilla he is assembling.

Postgraduate education has become a valuable asset in political career building. More than one-third of the national bureaucratic elite in 1984 held master's degrees, and both the de la Madrid and Salinas administrations had ample representation of persons at the cabinet and subcabinet levels who had earned doctorates at elite U.S. and European universities.[36]

Since the 1970s, kinship ties have also become more important as a common denominator of those who attain positions of political power. Increasingly, such people are born into politically prominent families that have already produced state governors, cabinet ministers, federal legislators, and even presidents. In 1987, all three of the leading precandidates for the PRI's presidential nomination, as well as opposition leader Cuauhtémoc Cárdenas, were *"cachorros"* (cubs)—the offspring of earlier, nationally known political figures. Family connections can give an aspiring political leader a powerful advantage over rivals. In effect, he inherits the camarilla that has been assembled by his politically prominent relative, and the relative himself becomes a key mentor and opener of doors. In short, "politics in Mexico has become a 'family affair.'"[37]

Despite the privileged social background of Mexico's post-revolutionary political elite, relatively few of its members have come from the country's wealthiest families. The offspring of such

---

[36]Centeno, "The New Científicos."

[37]Lorenzo Meyer, "Linajes políticos: Las buenas familias," *Excélsior* (Mexico City), October 27, 1982. See also: Smith, *Labyrinths of Power*, 307-10; Roderic Camp, "Family Relationships in Mexican Politics," *Journal of Politics* 44 (August 1982): 848-62.

families tended to pursue careers in private business rather than politics. Indeed, the upheaval of 1910-20 seems to have engendered two fairly distinct national elites—a political elite and an entrepreneurial elite—rather than a single "power elite" dominating both the political and economic arenas.[38] While the representation of persons with family or career ties to private capital within the national political elite has been increasing over the past twenty years, the incidence of public-/private-sector elite interlocks is still relatively low.[39] The two elites have often shared important interests and objectives, and for most of the period since 1940 they have worked in tandem to develop Mexico within a mixed-economy framework. However, recent sexenios have demonstrated that the public policy preferences and agendas of Mexico's political and business elites can and do diverge.[40]

The growing importance of political family dynasties and other indicators of increasing homogeneity in personal backgrounds has caused some observers to worry that Mexico's political elite is becoming more closed and inbred. While its social base may, indeed, be narrowing, the modern Mexican political elite stills shows considerable fluidity; the massive turnover of officeholders every six years is proof of that. The circulation of political elites in Mexico is not just a game of musical chairs. According to one tabulation, 80 percent of the top two hundred officeholders are replaced every twelve years and 90 percent every eighteen years. At the end of each administration, nearly one-third of the top-level players actually drop out of political life.[41] This helps to explain why in Mexico, unlike other postrevolutionary countries such as China and (until recently) the Soviet Union, the regime has not become a gerontocracy. The major exception to this rule is the national-level leadership of the government-controlled labor movement, which has been dominated since the 1940s by the same individuals.

---

[38]Smith, *Labyrinths of Power*, 213-15.

[39]One study of a sample of prominent Mexican entrepreneurs from the 1920s through the mid-1980s found that 15 percent had held national political office, while only 10 percent of cabinet-level public officials during the same period had had private-sector career experiences at the managerial level (Roderic A. Camp, *Entrepreneurs and Politics in Twentieth Century Mexico* [New York: Oxford University Press, 1989], 82).

[40]See Sylvia Maxfield and Ricardo Anzaldúa Montoya, eds., *Government and Private Sector in Contemporary Mexico*, Monograph Series, no. 20 (La Jolla, Calif.: Center for U.S.-Mexican Studies, University of California, San Diego, 1987); and Maxfield, *Governing Capital: International Finance and Mexican Politics* (Ithaca, N.Y.: Cornell University Press, 1990).

[41]Smith, *Labyrinths of Power*, chap. 6.

The movement of thousands of persons into and out of the ruling elite at regular intervals has been a key source of political stability in Mexico, because it reinforces the idea of "giving everyone a turn." At least at the highest levels of the system, members of the political elite remain in power for only a certain length of time. The implied lesson is that politically ambitious individuals will get their chance to acquire power, status, and wealth—if they are patient, persistent, and self-disciplined.

TÉCNICOS VERSUS POLÍTICOS

In recent sexenios, this calculus of expectations has been upset somewhat by the rise of the so-called técnicos. Beginning in the Echeverría administration, but especially in the de la Madrid and Salinas sexenios, persons whose careers have been built mainly in the arena of electoral politics and in the labor unions and peasant organizations affiliated with the ruling party have been eclipsed in the competition for high office.

They have increasingly lost out to the técnicos, whose main ticket of admission to the national political elite is an advanced university degree, often acquired abroad, in such disciplines as economics and public administration. Typically, the técnicos come from upper-class families and spend their entire careers within the government bureaucracy, especially the financial and planning agencies. They generally lack substantial personal constituencies outside the bureaucracy, because they have not had the opportunity or need to develop such followings. The vast majority of técnicos who make it to the highest levels of the system have not run for elective office. Carlos Salinas is the fourth man in a row to become president of Mexico without having held an elective office. Like Salinas, the most upwardly mobile técnicos increasingly get their only experience in party politics through a brief stint in the PRI's think tank (IEPES), where they write the party's platform and help run a presidential campaign. The técnicos rise to power far more rapidly than the average traditional político, on the strength of their expertise and problem-solving capacity in fields that are important to the government (e.g., public finance) and, especially, their camarilla ties.[42] Carlos Salinas, perhaps the quintessential técnico, was only thirty-four years old when he was appointed to a

---

[42]On the widening generational gap within Mexico's political elite, see Peter H. Smith, "Leadership and Change: Intellectuals and Technocrats in Mexico," in *Mexico's Political Stability: The Next Five Years*, ed. Roderic A. Camp (Boulder, Colo.: Westview, 1986), 101-17.

key cabinet post by President de la Madrid, and thirty-nine when he was nominated for the presidency (see figure 4).

The so-called traditional políticos are conspicuously older when they attain positions of power, because they typically have spent many years doing service for the PRI and/or its affiliated sectoral organizations. With the rise of the técnicos, the traditional políticos have found their access to the most important posts in the government blocked. They have also been saddled with a set of "antipopular" economic policies favored by the technocrats in power and with the responsibility of maintaining political control and electoral support for the PRI in a period of economic crisis and government austerity. Meanwhile, the técnicos have concentrated on fashioning new development strategies and negotiating foreign debt deals. Not surprisingly, during the 1980s this division of labor generated considerable tension between the técnicos and traditional politicians, especially since the career rewards for the políticos' efforts to win elections and mobilize mass support for the government's policies had been sharply diminished.

Traditional políticos have also been distressed by their lack of influence over the direction of public policy in recent sexenios. The técnicos have chosen to pursue an economic project emphasizing reduced government spending on subsidies to consumers, privatization of public enterprises, industrial "reconversion" or modernization, basing Mexican development more on a capacity to export, and timely servicing of the nation's external debt. Many traditional políticos objected to this neoliberal, outward-looking economic policy mix, arguing that its social costs were too high and that such policies would further undermine electoral support for the PRI. Fundamentally, the políticos have been apprehensive about the técnicos' preferred approach to development because it implies upsetting many of the internal economic and political arrangements that have evolved in Mexico since the 1930s under a more inward-looking, protectionist set of government policies. Finally, the políticos have been alarmed by the técnicos' plans to change the rules of the electoral game in ways that would make it more difficult for the políticos to do their jobs and to retain their traditional share of public positions. Old-guard PRI leaders feared a political opening and an increase in genuine competition, especially in the midst of an economic crisis, while some high-ranking técnicos—including, initially, Presidents de la Madrid and Salinas—pushed for "modernization" of the PRI and the electoral system. The resulting tensions contributed importantly to the breakdown in PRI unity that occurred in 1987-88, which gave rise

Figure 4
Career of Carlos Salinas de Gortari

1948: Born in Mexico City

Father, Raúl Salinas Lozano, studied engineering at Mexico's National University (UNAM) and economics at Harvard University; served as Secretary of Industry and Commerce under President Adolfo López Mateos (1958-64).

1967-71: Undergraduate study at UNAM

Majored in economics; took public administration courses from Miguel de la Madrid.

1970-78: Part-time university teaching

Taught at UNAM, Autonomous Technological Institute of Mexico (ITAM), and Center for Latin American Monetary Studies (CEMLA).

1971-74: Finance Ministry: Analyst, Office of International Financial Affairs

Appointed by Hugo Margáin (Treasury Secretary), who had been Undersecretary in the Ministry of Industry and Commerce when that ministry was headed by Raúl Salinas Lozano.

1972-74: Postgraduate study at Harvard and M.I.T.

Earned M.A. in public administration; M.A. and Ph.D. in political economy, completing his doctoral dissertation in 1978 (topic: relationships among public investment, political participation, and mass support for the government in rural areas of Puebla and Tlaxcala states).

1974-79: Finance Ministry

Held various positions, including Director, Dept. of Economics Studies, Office of International Financial Affairs; and Director General of Financial Planning. Worked under Miguel de la Madrid (Undersecretary of the Treasury) and José López Portillo (Treasury Secretary).

1979-81: Director of Economic and Social Policy, Ministry of Planning and Budget

Appointed by Miguel de la Madrid (Secretary of Planning and Budget).

1981-82: Director, Institute of Political, Economic, and Social Studies (IEPES), PRI

Ran the PRI's "think tank" during Miguel de la Madrid's presidential campaign; campaigned with de la Madrid throughout the country.

1982-87: Secretary of Planning and Budget

Appointed at age 34 — youngest member of the de la Madrid cabinet.

1987: Nominated as presidential candidate of the PRI

1988-94: President of Mexico

to the dissident candidacy of Cuauhtémoc Cárdenas and the PRI's electoral debacle of July 1988.

The dichotomy between técnicos and políticos undoubtedly has been overdrawn. The técnicos have been stereotyped as "number crunchers" whose abstract formulas for public policy do not take account of popular needs and frustrations, and who lack basic political skills. While some high-ranking technocrats could fairly be criticized for insensitivity to social realities, those who rise to the top of the government hierarchy today could not possibly achieve such positions by technical competence and administrative experience alone; they must be highly skilled political alliance builders as well. Their bureaucratic responsibilities often require them to negotiate deals with state governors and other prominent members of the traditional political class, who may be incorporated into a técnico's personal network of supporters. In the competition for higher office, "political technocrats" who have engaged in political activity (however briefly) have an important edge over those who lack such experience.

The técnico/político distinction is further blurred by the fact that many políticos perform management functions in the central PRI bureaucracy and general political control duties in Gobernación and other ministries. Like the técnicos, such "political bureaucrats" can make their careers without ever engaging directly in voter electoral mobilization or representation of one of the PRI's sectoral constituencies (peasants, organized labor, middle-class professionals, etc.).

Mexico's traditional politicians have clearly lost power during recent sexenios, but they have not been completely displaced. The cabinets chosen by Mexico's two most recent, technocratic presidents have been a blend of young técnicos (concentrated in the economic and planning ministries) and experienced politicians. The departments most critical to political control (such as Gobernación, Labor, and Education) have been left in the hands of older, career politicians regarded as hard-liners on matters of electoral politics and internal security. Salinas, in particular, made an effort to reach out to the traditional political class, choosing for his cabinet a substantial number of men who are highly skilled political brokers and who, by virtue of both age and experience, could serve as a bridge between Salinas's technocratic inner circle and the PRI's old guard. The proportion of Salinas cabinet members with some sort of political experience (especially having held state governorships) was more than double that of the preceding de la Madrid cabinet (see figure 5).

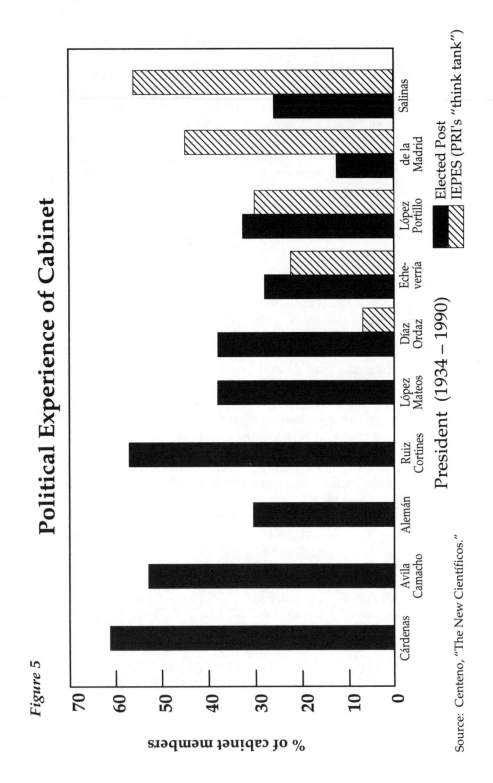

Figure 5

Political Experience of Cabinet

% of cabinet members

70 — 60 — 50 — 40 — 30 — 20 — 10 — 0

Cárdenas   Avila Camacho   Alemán   Ruiz Cortines   López Mateos   Díaz Ordaz   Eche-verría   López Portillo   de la Madrid   Salinas

President (1934 – 1990)

■ Elected Post
▨ IEPES (PRI's "think tank")

Source: Centeno, "The New Científicos."

Through his cabinet appointments and his go-slow approach to political reform, Salinas succeeded in reducing tensions within the national political elite. There is now a reasonably comfortable, symbiotic relationship between the two wings of the elite, rather than the barely concealed antagonism of the 1980s. The traditional políticos need the technocrats to run the economy and negotiate complex arrangements with the outside world; the técnicos need the políticos to maintain political control. Nevertheless, a significant and probably irreversible shift of power has occurred within Mexico's political elite. Career politicians must now implement decisions made by technocrats, whose approach to the country's problems places much less emphasis on traditional populism and economic nationalism, and who are more preoccupied with economic problem solving than with the health of the political system. Since future Mexican presidents are likely to be recruited from the ranks of the technocrats, there is little prospect of a return to government by traditional políticos.

Interest Representation and Political Control

In the Mexican system, important public policies are initiated and shaped by the inner circle of presidential advisers before they are even presented for public discussion. Most interest representation therefore takes place within the upper levels of the government bureaucracy. The structures that aggregate and articulate interests in Western democracies (political parties, labor unions, and so on) actually serve other purposes in the Mexican system: limiting the scope of citizens' demands on the government, mobilizing electoral support for the regime, helping to legitimate it in the eyes of other countries, distributing jobs and other material rewards to select individuals and groups. The principal vehicle for interest representation in the Mexican system, the official party PRI, has no independent influence on public policy; nor do the opposition parties in the system.

Since the late 1930s, Mexico has had a corporatist system of interest representation, in which each citizen and societal segment should relate to the state through one structure "licensed" by the state to organize and represent that sector of society (peasants, urban unionized workers, businessmen, teachers, etc.). The official party itself is divided into three sectors: the peasant sector, the labor sector, and the "popular" sector (representing most government employees, small merchants, private landowners, and low-income urban neighborhood groups). Each sector is dominated by one mass organization: the Confederación de Trabajadores de México (CTM) in the labor sector; the Confederación Nacional Campesina (CNC) in the peasant sector; and the Confederación Nacional de Organizaciones Populares (CNOP) in the popular sector. Other organizations are affiliated with each party sector, but their influence is dwarfed by that of the principal confederation.

A number of powerful organized interest groups—foreign and domestic entrepreneurs, the military, the Catholic church—also are not formally represented in the PRI. These groups deal directly with the governmental elite, often at the presidential or cabinet level; they do not need the PRI to make their preferences known. These groups also have well-placed representatives within the executive branch who can be counted upon to articulate their interests. In addition, the business community is organized into several government-chartered confederations (CONCA-NACO, CONCAMIN, CANACINTRA), which take positions on public issues and have their preferences widely disseminated through the mass media. Since the Cárdenas administration, all but a handful of the country's industrialists and businessmen have been required by law to join one of these employers' organizations. In the 1980s, several businessmen's organizations independent of the state-sanctioned associations (most notably, COPARMEX, the Confederación Patronal de la República Mexicana) took a leading role in criticizing government economic policies.[43]

Because the party system and the national legislature do not effectively aggregate interests in the Mexican system, numerous conflicting claims must be resolved directly by the president or by one of the several "super ministries" (such as Planning and Budget) that have been created within the executive branch to serve as coordinating mechanisms. Large numbers of poorly aggregated and conflicting demands can at times threaten to overwhelm the decision-making apparatus and induce paralysis. But this pattern of interest mediation is also functional in maintaining the system's stability.

Individuals and groups seeking something from the regime often circumvent their nominal representatives in the PRI sectoral organizations and seek satisfaction of their needs through personal contacts—patrons—within the governmental apparatus. These patron-client relationships compartmentalize the society into discrete, noninteracting, vertical segments that serve as pillars of the regime. Within the lower class, for example, unionized urban workers are separated from nonunion urban workers; ejidatarios from small private landholders and landless agricultural workers. The middle class is compartmentalized into government bureaucrats, educators, health care professionals, lawyers, economists, and so forth. Thus, competition between social classes is replaced by highly fragmented competition within classes.

---

[43]See Luis Felipe Bravo Mena, "COPARMEX and Mexican Politics," in *Government and Private Sector in Contemporary Mexico*, ed. Maxfield and Anzaldúa Montoya, 89-104.

The articulation of interests through patron-client networks assists the regime by reducing the number of potential beneficiaries for government programs and by limiting the scope of the demands made on the regime. It fragments popular demands into small-scale, highly individualized or localized requests that can be granted or denied case by case. Officials are rarely confronted with collective demands from broad social groupings. Rather than having to act on a request from a whole category of people (slum dwellers, ejidatarios, teachers), officials have easier, less costly choices to make (as between competing petitions from several neighborhoods for a piped water system).

The clientelistic structure not only provides a mechanism for distributing government benefits selectively; it also helps to legitimate such selectivity. It places the responsibility for outcomes upon individual patrons and clients. If community X fails to receive its school, it must be because its patron in the state government has failed to do his job, or because community residents themselves have not been skillful or persistent enough in cultivating enough patrons, or the right patrons, in the right government agencies—"the myth of the right connection."[44] This reasoning helps to limit citizens' frustration with government performance, while making it more difficult for dissident leaders to organize people on the basis of broadly shared economic grievances.

The appearance in recent years of independent organizations not tied into the regime's clientelistic networks has introduced new complexity and uncertainty into the political system. Numerous movements and organizations have emerged spontaneously among the urban poor, peasants, and even some middle-class groups like schoolteachers, which the PRI-government apparatus has generally failed to incorporate. These movements have developed partly in response to economic grievances created by the crisis, partly because of the declining responsiveness of existing state-chartered "mass" organizations to popular demands, and partly as a result of general societal modernization (expansion of mass communications, higher education levels, urbanization, changes in occupational structure, and the like). Because of the economic crisis and government austerity policies, state-affiliated organizations had little or nothing to deliver in terms of material benefits and were increasingly viewed by the Mexican people as instruments of manipulation and corrupt, self-serving extensions of the state bureaucracy. But the new popular movements have

---

[44]Evelyn P. Stevens, *Protest and Response in Mexico* (Cambridge, Mass.: MIT Press, 1974), 94.

been equally distrustful of the traditional opposition political parties. Until the late 1980s, they avoided collaborating with all parties operating at the national level, preferring to focus their energies on localized struggles for land, water, housing, and other improvements in urban barrios.[45] In the 1988 election, many popular organizations supported the presidential candidacy of Cuauhtémoc Cárdenas, and a large portion of movement adherents probably voted for him; but the movements' support for the Partido de la Revolución Democrática (PRD), the political party established by Cárdenas after the 1988 election, has been limited and sporadic. In some parts of Mexico (e.g., Oaxaca, Durango, Baja California), leaders of popular movements have begun to compete directly in elections for local positions of power.

There is lively debate among scholars and political practitioners in Mexico about the long-term significance of the new popular movements and, more generally, the political awakening of civil society. Some view the recent organizational dynamism of civil society as a watershed in Mexican history, providing evidence of a fundamental crisis of representation in the Mexican political system. For example, some of the earliest peasant movements that challenged the CNC developed because it simply had failed to provide effective representation of the campesinos' interests. Thus, the emergence of numerous, highly localized popular movements that are seemingly apolitical (at least beyond the arena of municipal politics) and that pursue their own agendas is a symptom of the breakdown of corporatist controls and of the increasing inability of the state-chartered mass organizations to incorporate newly emerging social sectors and interests into the official fold.

While intra-elite conflict and the scarcity of patronage resources contributed greatly to the decline of the corporatist system in the 1980s, developments in civil society threatened it in other ways. The continued growth of the middle class and its increasing propensity to organize around issues like environmental pollution and inadequate urban services; the burgeoning of an unorganized, politically unincorporated, "informally" employed segment of the low-income urban population (often referred to as *los marginados*); and a peasantry enraged by the depredations of natural resource exploiters, encroaching urban development, and credit squeezes by government banks—all have served as catalysts for the gradual emergence of a qualitatively new, more participant political cul-

---

[45]See Joe Foweraker and Ann L. Craig, eds., *Popular Movements and Political Change in Mexico* (Boulder, Colo.: Lynne Rienner, 1990); and Neil Harvey, *The New Agrarian Movement in Mexico, 1979-1990*, Monograph 23 (London: Institute of Latin American Studies, 1990).

ture. Mexico's political leaders now confront a substantially larger number of interest groups, pursuing their goals in a less deferential, more independent manner. There appears to have been sufficient popular mobilization during the 1980s to capture the attention of political elites, who now recognize—however grudgingly—the growing pluralism of civil society and the need to respond to it, perhaps by revitalizing corporatist structures or bypassing them through new forms of leadership and representation.[46]

Nevertheless, it must be recognized that while the Mexican regime's vaunted political control capabilities have been weakened by the economic and political crises of recent sexenios, the traditional instruments of control—patron-client relationships, *caciquismo* (local-level boss rule), the captive labor movement, selective repression of dissidents by government security forces—remain in place and have not lost all of their former effectiveness. The low incidence of protest behavior, unauthorized strikes, and other forms of civil disobedience in Mexico during the post-1982 period of mounting social pain suggests that the PRI-government apparatus remains highly skilled at dividing, buying off, co-opting, and—if necessary—repressing protest movements before they get out of hand.

PARTIDO REVOLUCIONARIO INSTITUCIONAL (PRI)

Mexico's "official" party, the Partido Revolucionario Institucional (PRI), was founded in 1929 by President Plutarco Calles to serve as a mechanism for reducing violent conflict among contenders for public office, and for consolidating the power of the central government, at the expense of the personalistic, local and state-level political machines that had passed for political parties during the decade following the 1910-20 Revolution. As historian Lorenzo Meyer has said, the official party was a party born "not to fight for power, but to administer it without sharing it."[47] For more than half a century the ruling party served with impressive efficiency as a mechanism for resolving elite conflicts, for co-opting newly emerging interest groups into the system, and for legitimating the regime through the electoral process. Potential defectors from the official party were deterred by the government's manipulation of

---

[46]See Wayne A. Cornelius, Judith Gentleman, and Peter H. Smith, "The Dynamics of Political Change in Mexico," in Cornelius, Gentleman, and Smith, eds., *Mexico's Alternative Political Futures*, Monograph Series, no. 30 (La Jolla, Calif: Center for U.S.-Mexican Studies, University of California, San Diego, 1989), 28-30.

[47]Lorenzo Meyer, "La democracia política: Esperando a Godot," *Nexos* 100 (April 1986): 42.

electoral rules, which made it virtually impossible for any dissident faction to bolt the party and win an election. Dissident movements did emerge in 1940, 1946, 1952, and 1987-88, but before the
neo-Cardenista coalition contested the 1988 election, no breakaway presidency candidacy had been able to garner more than 16
percent of the vote (by official count).

In 1938 President Lázaro Cárdenas transformed the official
party from an elite conflict-resolution/co-optation mechanism
into a mass-based political party that could be used explicitly to
build popular support for government policies and to mobilize
participation in elections. Cárdenas accomplished this by merging
into the official party the local, state, and national-level organizations of peasants and urban workers that had been created during
his presidency.[48] This reorganization established the party's claim
to be an inclusionary party, one that would seek to absorb into it as
many as possible of the diverse economic interests and political
tendencies that were represented in Mexican society. The official
party and its affiliated mass organizations occupied so much
political space that opposition parties and movements found it
difficult to recruit supporters.

From the beginning, the official party was an appendage of the
government itself, especially of the presidency. It was never a truly
independent arena of political competition. A handful of nationally powerful party leaders, such as Fidel Velázquez, patriarch of
the PRI-affiliated labor movement, occasionally constrained government actions, but the official party itself has never exerted any
independent influence on government economic and social policies. Indeed, one of the key sources of the tensions that led to the
breakdown of party unity and discipline in the late 1980s—culmi-
nating in the neo-Cardenista movement—was the PRI's lack of
autonomy from unpopular government austerity policies and the
inability of the party's most entrenched leaders and cadres to
influence the policy choices being made by the technocrats in the
government.

During the 1940s and '50s Mexico's ruling party became one
of the world's most accomplished vote-getting machines, guaran-
teeing an overwhelming victory at the polls for all but a handful of
its candidates in every election. None of the party's nominees for
president has ever been officially defeated, and until 1988-89 none
of its candidates for federal senator or state governor had been

---

[48]See Wayne A. Cornelius, "Nation-building, Participation, and Distribution: The
Politics of Social Reform under Cárdenas," in *Crisis, Choice, and Change: Historical
Studies of Political Development*, ed. Gabriel A. Almond et al. (Boston: Little, Brown,
1973), 392-498.

denied victory. Only since the 1970s have opposition parties been able to win appreciable numbers of municipal presidencies and seats in the lower house of Congress. By 1990, opposition parties controlled 5 percent of Mexico's nearly 2,400 municipal governments—up from 1 percent in 1985.

The official party has always had a number of major advantages over its electoral competitors. One is privileged access to the mass media (and particularly, since the 1960s, television). The media typically devote 90 percent or more of their coverage of electoral campaigns to the PRI's candidates, and the special political television broadcasts established by law to give opposition parties access to the media are scheduled at very low viewing hours, while the PRI invariably gets prime time.

The official party also enjoys essentially unlimited access to government funds to finance its campaigns. No one knows how much is actually transferred from government coffers to the PRI, since Mexico has no laws requiring the reporting of campaign income and expenditures. However, when an opposition government took power in the state of Baja California Norte, it found bank and legal records showing that more than U.S. $10 million in government funds had been channeled to the PRI for its 1989 gubernatorial campaign in that state. The PRI contends that it receives only the small government subsidy provided to all registered political parties under the terms of the federal electoral law, and dues from party members, which are typically deducted automatically from the salaries of government employees.

As the party in power, the PRI and its affiliated mass organizations have benefited from a vast network of government patronage, through which small-scale material benefits could be delivered to large segments of the population. The economic crisis of the 1980s and the government austerity measures it provoked sharply reduced the resources that could be pumped through that national patronage system. One reason for the PRI's loss of voter support as the crisis wore on was that it had become increasingly ineffectual in delivering material rewards. The fiscally conservative Salinas administration's solution to this problem has been to concentrate the resources available for government patronage in a smaller number of politically strategic localities and neighborhoods, especially the vote-rich urban slums where the neo-Cardenista movement won much of its support in 1988. Salinas's highly visible National Solidarity Program (PRONASOL) invests mainly in infrastructure that low-income Mexicans badly need (piped water, electricity, sewage systems, paved streets, medical clinics, housing). It requires community self-help in obtaining, installing, and paying for these improvements. It also emphasizes the linkage between the public goods provided and the government's policy of privatizing money-losing state-owned enterprises in order to free up revenues for PRONASOL and other social programs. PRONASOL has been criticized by opposition politicians as selective "neopopulism," but it represents a shrewd and potentially effective way to weaken the appeal of opposition parties and replenish the patronage resources of lower-level PRI functionaries.

The PRI is the only political party in Mexico that possesses a truly nationwide network of campaign organizers, local representatives, and poll watchers. It could count among its local cadres the one million members of the PRI-affiliated national teachers' union, who have played a particularly important role in securing the PRI's rural vote. The huge size and geographic dispersion of the ruling party's network of militants translate into great advantages at election time. For example, it would take over 100,000 poll watchers to cover every polling place in the country during a presidential election. None of the opposition parties can come remotely close to fielding this number of poll watchers. The PRI also has the manpower to get its voters to the polls—especially important in a period of rising abstentionism.

Historically, the official party's most potent advantage over the competition has been its ability to commit electoral fraud with relative impunity. A wide variety of techniques has been used: stuffing ballot boxes, intimidating potential opposition supporters by threatening to withdraw government benefits, disqualifying opposition party poll watchers, relocating polling places at the last minute to sites known only to PRI supporters, manipulating voter registration lists (padding them with nonexistent or nonresident PRIistas while "shaving" those who might vote against the ruling party from the rolls), issuing multiple voting credentials to PRI supporters, organizing multiple voting by *carruseles* ("flying brigades" of PRI supporters transported from one polling place to the next), and so forth. Moreover, with majority representation in all of the local, state, and national government committees that control polling and vote counting, the PRI has always been able to count on "electoral alchemy" to nullify unfavorable election outcomes or manipulate the tallies to deny victory to opposition candidates. Final results have been determined from above, sometimes through secret negotiations with the opposition parties, more often by fiat.[49]

The extent of fraud has varied greatly from region to region and from one election to another. In isolated, predominantly agrarian states that have no major cities (Tabasco, Campeche, Quintana Roo), the official party's candidates have often been credited with nearly 100 percent of the votes. Most historians have concluded that massive fraud was needed to impose Manuel Avila Camacho as victor in the 1940 presidential election. In recent decades, opposition party victories for several state governorships and municipal presidencies of large cities seem to have occurred but were not recognized by PRI-dominated electoral commissions.

Fraud has become such an integral part of the electoral process over the years that its sudden removal could produce disastrous results for the PRI. During the first ten months of Miguel de la Madrid's presidency, the government followed a policy of recognizing municipal-level victories by opposition party candidates wherever they occurred. The PRI was soon forced to concede defeat to the PAN in seven major cities, including five state capitals. Under intense pressure from alarmed and angry state and local PRI leaders, de la Madrid abruptly suspended his policy of "electoral transparency," and during the remainder of his term only one relatively small city was allowed to pass into opposition control.

Until recently, the weakness of opposition parties made it possible for the PRI-government apparatus to control election outcomes without blatant rigging. Indeed, in most parts of the country, the PRI's candidates for president, governor, and federal senator would probably have won an absolute majority of the votes even if no doctoring of election results had occurred. Beginning in 1985, however, gubernatorial and municipal elections in a number of states (Sonora, Chihuahua, Baja California Norte, Michoacán, Guerrero, México State) produced such an avalanche of opposition votes that tallies could not be adjusted so inconspicuously. The costs of "electoral alchemy" had gone up. Such tactics now provoked postelection protest demonstrations, violent clashes between PRI and opposition party militants, extensive criticism in the international media, rising public cynicism, and higher abstention in subsequent elections. In the case of Baja Cali-

---

[49]For examples, see Silvia Gómez-Tagle, "Democracia y poder en México: El significado de los fraudes electorales en 1979, 1982 y 1985," *Nueva Antropología* 9:3 (1986): 127-57; and George Philip, "The Dominant Party System in Mexico," in *Political Parties in the Third World*, ed. Vicky Randall (Newbury Park, Calif.: Sage, 1988), 107-108.

fornia Norte in 1989, national-level PRI and government authorities apparently concluded that the cost of blatant cheating would be excessive, and the PAN's historic state-level victory was recognized. In other states, heavy-handed electoral manipulations have persisted, with or without the sanction of central authorities.

While there was no effective opposition, the PRI's approach was to do everything possible to boost voter turnout, thus enabling the official party to roll up the huge majorities needed to validate its right to rule. With the emergence of strong opposition, blanket exhortations to register and vote have been replaced by a more targeted, block-by-block strategy aimed at mobilizing only those voters most likely to vote for the PRI. The presence of new opposition forces in the countryside—most notably, the neo-Cardenistas—has also constrained the PRI's ability to add votes to its totals, thereby artificially inflating voter participation. Such adding of votes to the PRI column, rather than taking votes away from opposition parties, has been the most common form of electoral fraud in rural areas. The effects of these changes can be seen in sharply reduced voter turnout rates since the late 1980s, even in hotly contested elections: no higher than 49.4 percent in the 1988 presidential election (see table 1); 15-33 percent in several key state and local elections held in 1989 and 1990.[50]

The share of the vote claimed by the PRI has been declining for nearly thirty years, but until recently the decline has been gradual and has not threatened the party's grasp on the presidency and state governorships (see figure 6 and table 2). The proportion of electoral districts dominated by the PRI dropped from 85 percent in 1964 to 35 percent in 1988 (see the first three columns of table 3). In 1988 opposition parties officially defeated the PRI in nearly 23 percent of the country's three hundred electoral districts. In terms of expressed party preference, opinion surveys suggest that the PRI had ceased to be a majority party by 1987, when less than 30

---

[50]Voter turnout in states and municipalities where elections have been held since 1988 has been lower than in previous, subnational elections in the same states and localities. Of course, other factors have also contributed to lower turnout rates. For example, persistent, increasingly visible vote fraud undermines the credibility of the opposition parties' challenge and reinforces feelings of powerlessness and cynicism among the general public ("No matter who you vote for, the PRI always wins"). This makes it much more difficult for the opposition to get out its vote. Any explanation of the trend toward higher abstentionism must be speculative, however, since there has been virtually no systematic research on nonvoting in Mexico.

Table 1
Voting in Presidential Elections, 1934-1988

Year	Votes for PRI Candidate[a] (%)	Votes for PAN Candidate (%)	Votes for All Others[b] (%)	Turnout (% Voters among Eligible Adults)[c]
1934	98.2	—	1.8	53.6
1940	93.9	—	6.1	57.5
1946	77.9	—	22.1	42.6
1952	74.3	7.8	17.9	57.9
1958	90.4	9.4	0.2	49.4
1964	88.8	11.1	0.1	54.1
1970	83.3	13.9	1.4	63.9
1976[d]	93.6	—	1.2	59.6
1982	71.0	15.7	9.4	66.1
1988	50.7	16.8	32.5[e]	49.4[f]

[a]From 1958 through 1982, includes votes cast for the Partido Popular Socialista (PPS) and the Partido Auténtico de la Revolución Mexicana (PARM), both of which regularly endorsed the PRI's presidential candidate. In 1988 they supported opposition candidate Cuauhtémoc Cárdenas.

[b]Excludes annulled votes; includes votes for candidates of nonregistered parties.

[c]Eligible population base for 1934 through 1952 includes all males ages 20 and over (legal voting age: 21 years). Both men and women aged 20 and over are included in the base for 1958 and 1964 (women received the franchise in 1958). The base for 1970-88 includes all males and females aged 18 and over (the legal voting age was lowered to 18, effective 1970).

[d]The PRI candidate, José López Portillo, ran virtually unopposed because the PAN failed to nominate a candidate. The only other significant candidate was Valentín Campa, representing the Communist Party, which was not legally registered to participate in the 1976 election. More than 5 percent of the votes were annulled.

[e]Includes 31.1 percent officially tabulated for Cuauhtémoc Cárdenas.

[f]Estimated using data from the Federal Electoral Commission. However, the Commission itself has released two different figures for the number of eligible voters in 1988. Using the Commission's larger estimate of eligible population, the turnout would be 44.9 percent.

Sources: Pablo González Casanova, *Democracy in Mexico* (New York: Oxford University Press, 1970), table 1; Peter H. Smith, *Labyrinths of Power* (Princeton, N.J.: Princeton University Press, 1979), table 2-7; Comisión Federal Electoral, *Procesos federales electorales, Cómputo de la votación por partido* (1964-88).

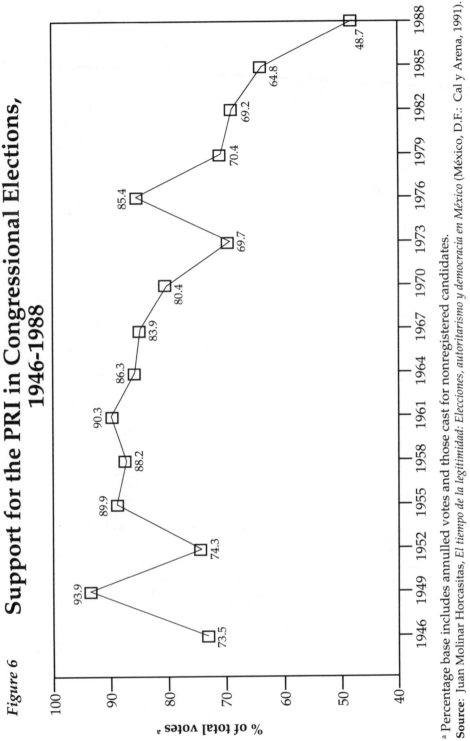

Figure 6   **Support for the PRI in Congressional Elections, 1946-1988**

[a] Percentage base includes annulled votes and those cast for nonregistered candidates.

Source: Juan Molinar Horcasitas, *El tiempo de la legitimidad: Elecciones, autoritarismo y democracia en México* (México, D.F.: Cal y Arena, 1991).

Table 2
Representation of Political Parties in Chamber of Deputies, 1964-1988
(percentage of seats)

Party	Year of Congressional Elections								
	1964	1967	1970	1973	1976	1979	1982	1985	1988
Partido Revolucionario Institucional (PRI)	83.3	82.1	83.6	82.2	82.0	82.2	74.8	72.3	52.0
Partido de Acción Nacional (PAN)	9.5	9.4	9.4	10.8	8.5	10.0	12.5	10.3	20.2
Partido Popular Socialista (PPS)[a]	4.8	4.7	4.7	4.3	5.1	2.8	2.5	2.8	(see FDN)
Partido Auténtico de la Revolución Mexicana (PARM)[a]	2.4	2.4	2.3	3.0	3.8	3.0	0.0	2.8	(see FDN)
Partido Democrático Mexicano (PDM)	—	—	—	—	—	2.5	3.0	3.0	0.0
Partido Socialista de los Trabajadores (PST)[a] (which became:) Partido del Frente Cardenista de Reconstrucción Nacional (PFCRN)	—	—	—	—	—	2.5	2.8	3.0	(see FDN)
Partido Comunista Mexicano (PCM) (which became:) Partido Socialista Unificado de México (PSUM) (which became:) Partido Mexicano Socialista (PMS)[b]	—	—	—	—	—	4.5	4.3	3.0	3.8
Partido Revolucionario de los Trabajadores (PRT)	—	—	—	—	—	—	0.0	1.5	0.0
Frente Democrático Nacional (FDN)[c]	—	—	—	—	—	—	—	—	24.0

[a]Party allied with the PRI before 1988.

[b]Party allied with the Cardenista front (FDN) in 1988.

[c]Coalition consisting of the PARM, PFCRN, and PPS. While these parties supported the same presidential candidate in 1988, Cuauhtémoc Cárdenas, they have not necessarily voted as a bloc in the Chamber of Deputies, especially since the formation of the Partido de la Revolución Democrática (PRD), the new Cardenista party, in 1989.

Source: Juan Molinar Horcasitas, El tiempo de la legitimidad: Elecciones, autoritarismo y democracia en México (México, D.F.: Cal y Arena, 1991).

Table 3
Patterns of Electoral Competition, 1964-1988
(percentage of 300 federal electoral districts)

Election year	PRI monopoly	Strong PRI hegemony	Weak PRI hegemony	Type of competition[a] Two-party competition	Multiparty competition	Opposition victory
1964	28.1	52.2	4.5	14.0	—	1.1
1967	24.2	61.2	3.6	9.7	—	1.2
1970	27.0	53.9	1.7	17.4	—	—
1973	18.7	51.3	4.1	21.8	1.0	3.1
1976	35.8	44.6	6.7	11.9	0.5	0.5
1979	9.4	48.0	12.3	6.3	22.7	1.3
1982	1.3	51.7	6.3	26.1	14.0	0.3
1985	3.3	41.7	9.0	21.0	21.3	3.7
1988[b]	1.0	19.0	15.0	8.3	34.0	22.7

[a] PRI monopoly = PRI vote > 95 percent; strong PRI hegemony = PRI vote < 95 percent but > 70; weak PRI hegemony = PRI vote < 70 percent but the difference between PRI and second party in district is > 40 percentage points; two party competition = PRI vote < 70 percent, difference between PRI and second party is < 40 percentage points, second party vote > 25 percent, and third party vote < 10 percent; multiparty competition = PRI vote < 70, difference between PRI and second party is < 40 percentage points, and second party vote < 25 percent or third party vote > 10 percent; opposition victory = any party's vote > PRI vote.

[b] For 1988, opposition victories include those won by the Cardenista coalition of parties.

Source: Leopoldo Gómez and John Bailey, "La transición política y los dilemas del PRI," Foro Internacional 31:1 (July-September 1990): 69.

Figure 7

PRI Performance in the 1988 Presidential Election

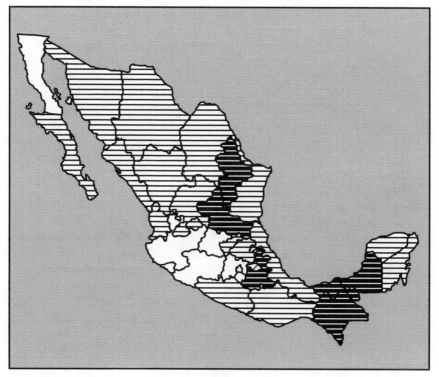

PRI DOMINANT (70-100%)

Campeche
Chiapas
Nuevo León
Puebla
Tabasco
San Luis Potosí

PRI MINORITY (<50%)

Baja Cal. Norte
Colima
Distrito Federal
Guanajuato
Jalisco
México State
Michoacán
Morelos

PRI COMPETITIVE (50-70%)

Aguascalientes	Querétaro
Baja Cal. Sur	Quintana Roo
Coahuila	Sinaloa
Chihuahua	Sonora
Durango	Tamaulipas
Guerrero	Tlaxcala
Hidalgo	Veracruz
Nayarit	Yucatán
Oaxaca	Zacatecas

Source: Miguel Angel Centeno, *Mexico in the 1990s: Government and Opposition Speak Out* (La Jolla, Calif.: Center for U.S.-Mexican Studies, UCSD, 1991).

percent of a national sample of Mexicans identified themselves as PRI supporters.[51]

One of the key factors accounting for the long-term decline in the official party's effectiveness as a vote-getting machine is the massive shift of population from rural to urban areas that has occurred in Mexico since 1950. In that year, 57 percent of the population lived in isolated rural communities of fewer than 2,500 inhabitants. By 1980, less than 34 percent lived in such localities, while 41 percent of all Mexicans lived in cities of 100,000 or more inhabitants. In large urban centers the regime's traditional mechanisms of political control work less efficiently. Education and income levels are higher, and the middle classes—which provide a considerable share of the opposition vote—are larger. The opposition parties are better organized and have more poll watchers in these places, making it more difficult for the PRI to conceal vote fraud. The data assembled in table 4 reveal that the PRI's electoral fortunes have declined most precipitously in the Mexico City metropolitan area (which now contains 25 percent of Mexico's total population) and other urban centers. In the 1988 presidential election, the would-be modernizer of Mexico, Carlos Salinas, derived his margin of victory from the most traditional, underdevel-

Table 4

Support for the PRI by Type of Congressional District
(percentage of total vote)

Districts	1979	1982	1985	1988	Average 1979-1988
Federal District (Mexico City)	46.7	48.3	42.6	27.3	41.2
Other Urban[a]	53.4	56.2	51.1	34.3	48.8
Mixed[b]	67.9	66.2	59.2	46.4	60.0
Rural[c]	83.5	80.9	77.3	61.3	75.8

[a]Urban districts are those in which 90 percent or more of the population lives in communities of 50,000 or more inhabitants. Total number: 40 in the Federal District and 56 in other urban areas.
[b]Districts in which more than 50 percent but less than 90 percent of the population lives in communities of 50,000 or more inhabitants. Total number: 44.
[c]Districts in which less than 50 percent of the population lives in communities of 50,000 inhabitants. Total number: 160.
Source: Molinar Horcasitas, *El tiempo de la legitimidad.*

[51]Miguel Basáñez, *El pulso de los sexenios: 20 años de crisis en México* (México, D.F.: Siglo Veintiuno, 1990), 276. In four subsequent national opinion surveys, conducted by Mexican and U.S. survey research organizations between June 1988 and June 1990, the proportion of respondents expressing a preference for the PRI ranged from 23 to 39 percent. (Data provided by the Centro de Estudios de Opinión Pública, Mexico City.)

oped parts of the country. He received only one out of four votes cast in Mexico City, while Cuauhtémoc Cárdenas took 49 percent of the vote there. Even in rural areas, however, opposition forces—primarily the neo-Cardenistas—have cut into the PRI's formerly "safe" vote.

Elections held in the 1980s were also marked by the collapse of the PRI's so-called sectoral vote—votes supposedly controlled by the party's affiliated campesino, labor, and "popular" (urban-middle-class and slum-dweller) organizations. For the 1988 election, the national peasant confederation promised to deliver ten million votes to the PRI's presidential candidate; the federation of public employees' unions promised two million votes; and the national teachers' union pledged that each of its one million members would mobilize a dozen or more voters for the PRI. The election results (Salinas was credited with a total of 9,687,926 votes, nearly five million fewer than PRI candidate Miguel de la Madrid received in 1982) dramatically demonstrated that the PRI could no longer rely on its sectoral organizations to deliver most of the votes needed to credibly win strongly contested national elections. Among the party's three sectors, organized labor performed most poorly (PRI candidates affiliated with that sector won a majority of the votes in only one-third of the electoral districts), while the "popular" sector was most effective in winning support for the PRI.[52] In general, however, the PRI's sectoral organizations now appear to have very little effective control over how their members vote.

Another major part of the PRI's dilemma is a massive generational shift in the electorate. The median age of the Mexican population today is about seventeen years. With each election, there are fewer Mexicans—particularly in the critical urban centers—who personally experienced the social reforms implemented in the 1930s, or even the post-1940 era of sustained economic growth and low inflation. Instead, today's under-35 voters have experienced fifteen years of recurrent economic crises, declining living standards, increasing inequality in wealth distribution, and political stagnation within the PRI-government apparatus. As a result, one of the most formidable challenges facing the PRI is how to stimulate loyalty to the party among the millions of first-time voters who are coming of age at a time of severely diminished rather than expanding economic opportunities.

---

[52]Guadalupe Pacheco Méndez, "Estructura y resultados electorales," *Examen* 2:15 (August 15, 1990): 20.

The magnitude of the PRI's so-called generational problem is suggested by several public opinion surveys showing that the ruling party's support is concentrated increasingly in the older age groups, while the opposition parties draw considerably more of their support from younger voters. A national preelection survey in 1988 found that more than 50 percent of the Cardenista coalition's support base consisted of persons under thirty years of age, while 42 percent of the PANista base and only 35 percent of the PRIistas were in this age group.[53] In the state of Chihuahua, the PRI receives the bulk of its support from people above age forty-three, while the youngest age groups (eighteen to thirty-two years) are dominated by PAN supporters.[54] The already substantial segment of the population that is dissatisfied with the PRI and inclined to support an opposition party will grow in the years to come, as the PRIista "old guard" dies off, particularly in rural areas, where the average age of the remaining population is rising rapidly. This has major implications for the PRI, since today it is the rural areas that continue to provide the winning margin for its candidates in many states.

Finally, the deep divisions that emerged within Mexico's political elite during the 1980s have impaired the PRI's performance in recent elections. Executive power has fallen increasingly into the hands of technocrats whose political style and experience differ sharply from that of old-line PRI bureaucrats. When the traditional políticos complain that the PRI apparatus is in bad shape today, the finger of blame is often pointed at technocrats like de la Madrid and Salinas, who allegedly allowed themselves to be consumed by the challenges of economic crisis management and restructuring, neglecting the task of revitalizing the official party even as they saddled the PRI with a set of conservative economic policies that were almost impossible to reconcile with decades of ruling party rhetoric and ideology. In his letter of resignation from the PRI, Cardenista leader Porfirio Muñoz-Ledo, a former national chairman of the party, charged that the technocrat-dominated PRI had "turned its back on the masses." The designation of Carlos Salinas as the PRI's presidential candidate in 1987 was taken by the nationalist-populist wing of the PRI as evidence that the government's economic policies would continue to shift to the right of

[53]PEAC (Prospectiva Estratégica, A.C.), "Encuesta I: El país/Distrito Federal," *Perfil de La Jornada*, July 5, 1988.

[54]Tonatiuh Guillén López, "Political Parties and Political Attitudes in Chihuahua," in *Electoral Patterns and Perspectives in Mexico*, ed. Arturo Alvarado, Monograph Series, no. 22 (La Jolla, Calif.: Center for U.S.-Mexican Studies, University of California, San Diego, 1987), 225-45.

Mexico's "revolutionary creed," and as a signal that the party's left wing would be reduced to permanent obsolescence and irrelevance.

The departure of the center-left Cardenistas from the PRI and their unexpectedly strong electoral showing in 1988 further polarized the situation, provoking a strong defensive response from the most conservative, politically hard-line elements within the PRI (represented by its labor sector). The hard-liners' demands for a crackdown on opposition groups—both within and outside of the PRI—and their insistence on winning elections at all costs exacerbated the long-running conflict within the political elite between those advocating some sort of political liberalization and those favoring the status quo. These developments have made it increasingly difficult for the PRI to function as a mechanism for elite conflict resolution, and they have handed the opposition parties by far their most effective campaign issue: persistent, highly visible vote fraud by the PRI.

OPPOSITION PARTIES

Until recently, the opposition parties essentially performed a stabilizing function in the Mexican political system. They gave the regime a loyal opposition in the Congress; provided an outlet for the protest vote (people so dissatisfied with the government's performance that they could not bring themselves to vote for PRI candidates); and served as vehicles for dissident political leaders, keeping them within the government-sanctioned arena of political competition. Internally fragmented and organizationally weak, the opposition parties could not attract sufficient electoral support to challenge PRI hegemony at the state or national levels. Leaders of these parties accepted seats in the Congress, criticized occasional policy decisions, and negotiated election results with the PRI-government apparatus. Their most basic function was to give the PRI something to run against, thereby strengthening the government's claim to popular support and legitimate authority.

The regime's basic strategy for dealing with the opposition parties was to "carry a big stick, and offer small carrots."[55] The carrots took the form of periodic tinkering with the federal election laws, so as to guarantee some level of representation for opposition parties in the Congress, make it easier for them to qualify for legal registration, and provide modest amounts of public financing for their campaigns. By tolerating opposition parties and en-

---

[55]Juan Molinar Horcasitas, *El tiempo de la legitimidad: Elecciones, autoritarismo y democracia en M xico* (México, D.F.: Cal y Arena, 1991), 63.

couraging the formation of additional ones, the regime was able to channel most of the public discontent with its policies and performance through the electoral process, rather than risking violent antisystem protests.

In the late 1970s, and especially since 1985, a less collaborationist electoral opposition emerged. Benefiting from the tidal wave of antigovernment sentiment provoked by the economic crisis of the 1980s, opposition parties of the right and left became more formidable competitors. Particularly on the right, the opposition sought mass support cutting across all social classes, hired full-time staff, and started conducting campaigns to win rather than simply educate the citizenry. Opposition parties of both right and left became more willing to adopt civil disobedience and other confrontational tactics in their dealings with the government, especially to protest electoral fraud. They began appealing to the international media, the Organization of American States, and even the U.S. Congress to validate their claims of victory. Their representatives in the Congress challenged key national policies, such as the nationalization of the banking system in 1982, the continued servicing of Mexico's huge external debt, and accelerated economic integration with the United States. In these ways they have disputed the government's legitimacy, embarrassed it abroad, and raised the cost of political control and co-optation.

Nevertheless, opposition parties in Mexico continue to operate under severe constraints. Limited access to the mass media, lack of control over patronage resources, and PRI-government control over the machinery of elections are among the most significant. It remains extremely difficult for opposition parties to "prove" electoral fraud; the evidentiary tests prescribed by the electoral code are severe. As a result, an opposition party cannot demand that its victories be recognized officially; it can only try to pressure the government (e.g., through public demonstrations) and *negotiate* particular victories behind closed doors.[56]

Electoral fraud works against the opposition parties in other ways too. By campaigning mainly against vote fraud, the opposition parties leave themselves open to the charge that they have no credible, alternative program for solving the economic and social problems afflicting the electorate. The continued fixation on fraud also causes many potential opposition party supporters to stay home when elections are held; they become disillusioned, no longer believing that opposition candidates have any reasonable

---

[56]Larissa A. Lomnitz, Claudio Lomnitz, and Ilya Adler, "El fondo de la forma: La campaña presidencial del PRI en 1988," *Nueva Antropología* 11:38 (1990): 62.

chance of winning. Public distrust of the electoral process hurts the opposition parties more than the PRI, which has the resources to get out its vote.

The principal opposition party on the right, the Partido de Acción Nacional (PAN), is the best equipped to overcome these handicaps. Established in 1939, the PAN has worked diligently to develop a nationwide, mass following and a strong network of militants capable of closely monitoring the electoral process and defending its vote. In its regional strongholds—the northern border states, Jalisco and Guanajuato states, the Mexico City metropolitan area (México State and the Federal District), and the Yucatán—it is able to roll up convincing majorities in major cities, even with extensive fraud by the PRI. The PAN is widely believed to have won or come very close to winning the gubernatorial elections in the states of Sonora in 1985 and Chihuahua in 1986. Its overwhelming, officially recognized gubernatorial victory in Baja California Norte in 1989 demonstrated that in at least some parts of the country, the PAN is sufficiently popular and well-organized to break PRI control over state governments. In these places, the PAN has managed to create a de facto two-party system. Its candidates for the federal Congress have been increasingly successful, taking 101 out of the 240 seats in the Chamber of Deputies that went to opposition party representatives in the 1988 elections—the largest number of seats ever won by a single opposition party.

The PAN was formed largely in reaction to the leftward drift of public policy under President Lázaro Cárdenas. Its founders included prominent Catholic intellectuals who espoused a Christian Democratic ideology, and the party has maintained its opposition to the anticlerical provisions of the 1917 Constitution, especially the government's monopoly over public education. In some parts of the country, Catholic priests have sided openly with the PAN, while criticizing electoral fraud committed by the PRI. The PAN's principal constituency is the urban middle classes, but it has also attracted votes among socially conservative peasants and the urban working class.

While clearly the leader among Mexico's opposition parties in terms of organizational strength and ideological coherence, the PAN is a party with several major weaknesses. Since the mid-1970s it has been divided into moderate-progressive and militant-conservative ("neo-PANista") factions, which have jockeyed for control of the party machinery and carried out purges of opposing faction members when they were in power. The PAN has few leaders of national stature, and it has had difficulty defining a national project or set of policies that constitutes a clear alternative

to the government's programs. This problem has been com-
pounded by the rightward shift in government policies since 1982.
Under de la Madrid and Salinas, the PAN has seen many of its
banners (free market-oriented economic policies, privatization of
state-owned enterprises, closer ties with the United States, improved church-state relations) stolen by the government.

In recent years, the divisions within the PAN have been wid-
ened by the willingness of the currently dominant (moderate)
party leadership to make tactical alliances with the Salinas government in order to pass constitutional amendments on such issues as
electoral law reform and reprivatization of the banks, in exchange
for assurances of cleaner elections. The persistence of PRI fraud in
PAN strongholds has denied the party many of its expected victories and made the PAN's national leaders vulnerable to challenges
from within their own party. Elections since 1988 have shown that
the PAN is holding onto its traditional constituency (now about 20
percent of the electorate) but not expanding it appreciably. In the
1988 presidential election, the neo-Cardenista movement cut
deeply into the PAN's usual antigovernment protest vote, especially among the urban poor.

Empirical research on PAN supporters has shown that the
party has a well-scrubbed, relatively privileged clientele that
wants to see the middle class recover from the ravages of the
economic crisis of the 1980s but is not much concerned about
absolute poverty, social inequality, or even broader participatory
democracy. By proportions ranging from 25 to 37 percent, PAN-
istas interviewed in one study conducted in a middle-class neighborhood of Mexico City believed that illiterates, leftists, Indians,
and the unemployed do not have the same rights as other citizens,
because they are not sufficiently prepared for democracy.[57] Such
findings suggest that a significant portion of the PAN's present
constituency is likely to be alienated by any future attempt by the
party to expand its base by embracing the unwashed masses.
There is also a significant "message" problem: it will be difficult
for the PAN to convince the masses that it is on their side until it
begins to address the country's social problems much more ag-
gressively and convincingly than it did in the 1988 election.

That election proved to be a dramatic turning point in the
fortunes of the leftist opposition in Mexico. Before 1988, the Mexican left had spawned political parties like the Partido Popular

---

[57]María Luisa Tarrés, "La oposición política y la idea de democracia entre las clases
medias en la coyuntura actual," in Soledad Loaeza and Claudio Stern, eds., *Las clases
medias en la coyuntura actual*, Cuadernos del CES, no. 33 (México, D.F.: El Colegio de
México, 1990), 85-86.

Socialista (PPS), which served for decades as a home for moderate socialists and other left-of-center politicians willing to collaborate with the government and even to endorse the PRI's presidential candidates, in exchange for a seat in Congress. The more independent left—that is, those who did not collaborate openly with the ruling party—was traditionally represented by the Partido Comunista Mexicano (PCM). The Communists were allowed to compete legally in elections during the presidency of Lázaro Cárdenas, but their party was subsequently outlawed and did not regain its legal registration until 1979, when its congressional candidates won 5 percent of the vote. During most of the 1980s, even in the face of Mexico's gravest economic crisis since the 1910 Revolution and despite a series of party mergers intended to reduce the fractionalization of the leftist vote, the parties to the left of the PRI lost ground electorally. They were hampered by constant internal squabbling (motivated by personalistic rivalries as well as ideological cleavages), an inability to do effective grassroots organizing, and an identification with discredited statist policies, now blamed for Mexico's economic debacle.

The key to the left's rejuvenation in 1988 was a split within the PRI leadership—the most serious since the early 1950s. In August 1986, a number of nationally prominent PRI figures, all members of the party's center-left wing, formed a dissident movement within the PRI known as the Corriente Democrática (CD). They were led by Porfirio Muñoz-Ledo (former head of the PRI, runner-up candidate for the party's presidential nomination in 1976, former secretary of labor and secretary of education), and Cuauhtémoc Cárdenas, who was just finishing his term as governor of the state of Michoacán. The CD criticized the de la Madrid administration's economic restructuring program and sought a renewed commitment by the PRI to traditional principles of economic nationalism and social justice. Most urgently, CD adherents called for a thoroughgoing "democratization" of the PRI, beginning with the elimination of the *dedazo* (unilateral selection by the outgoing president) as the mechanism for determining the party's presidential candidates. The CD's proposals were widely interpreted as a last-ditch attempt by the PRI's traditional políticos to recover leadership of the party by influencing the outcome of the 1987-88 presidential succession. The CD's demands for reform were resoundingly rejected by the PRI hierarchy and they formally split from the party in October 1987.

Confronted with defeat within the PRI, Cuauhtémoc Cárdenas accepted the presidential nomination of the Partido Auténtico de la Revolución Mexicana (PARM), a conservative, nationalist party established by another group of dissident PRIistas in 1954. Later, four other parties—all to the left of the PRI, and including the remnants of the old Mexican Communist Party—joined the PARM to form a coalition, the Frente Democrático Nacional (FDN), to contest the 1988 presidential election, with Cárdenas as their candidate. In its decision to join the neo-Cardenista coalition, and subsequently to become part of the new political party established by Cárdenas after the 1988 election, Mexico's independent left subordinated ideology to pragmatic considerations. Cuauhtémoc Cárdenas is not a socialist but rather a European-style social democrat. Before joining this coalition, the leftist parties had been attracting only insignificant support in public opinion polls, and some were in danger of losing their legal registration. As members of a center-left coalition led by a political figure with broad popular appeal, they stood to gain a great deal.

The neo-Cardenista movement posed a much stronger challenge to the PRI than any defection from that party since 1940.[58] It was particularly threatening because Cárdenas had considerable appeal to rank-and-file labor union members and campesinos—two of the PRI's traditional mass constituencies, which had benefited greatly from the social reforms implemented by President Lázaro Cárdenas. Moreover, many of the PRI's lower-echelon militants also sympathized with the nationalist-populist policies advocated by Cárdenas and his movement. There is even evidence that in the 1988 election, old-guard PRI leaders in some regions worked to turn out the vote for Cárdenas, as a protest against the reign of technocrats like Salinas.

Following the 1988 presidential election, the left's deeply ingrained tradition of internal factionalism reasserted itself. Cárdenas invited his FDN coalition partners to merge themselves into a new political party, the Partido de la Revolución Democrática (PRD), but several of them chose not to join. The former coalition partners do not necessarily vote together in the Congress. And serious divisions have emerged within the PRD's top leadership over such issues as the degree of democracy in internal party governance and strategies for dealing with the government ("dialogue" vs. "permanent confrontation").

The PRD continues to take policy positions to the left of the ruling party on some issues (e.g., arguing for a moratorium or cap on external debt service and a go-slow approach to economic integration with the United States); but the PRD has had difficulty

---

[58]The previous two breakaway movements ("Almazanismo" in 1940 and "Henriquismo" in 1952) won only 5.7 and 15.9 percent (respectively) of the presidential vote, according to official results.

in developing a general program that clearly differentiates it from its competitors. The PRD shares with the PRI and the PAN an emphasis on improving social conditions through economic growth, as opposed to redistribution of wealth; and its differences with most of the incumbent government's policies are matters of degree and pacing rather than substance.[59]

Like the PAN, the PRD is much stronger in some regions than in others. Its strongholds are the states of Michoacán, Guerrero, and Oaxaca, and the Mexico City metropolitan area. The PRD has retained the urban voters who supported the parties of the independent left, but as noted above it has also begun to take votes from the PRI in rural areas. It has begun to develop ties with the new popular movements that have emerged outside of the PRI-affiliated corporatist structures. The PRD's greatest challenge is to develop a well-institutionalized party structure, one that is not dependent on the personal charisma of Cuauhtémoc Cárdenas to mobilize PRD supporters and is strong enough to defend the PRD vote against PRI-government tactics of fraud and intimidation. State and local elections held since 1988 have shown that when Cárdenas himself is not on the ballot, support for the PRD falls off dramatically.[60] Under Salinas, the government has shown a greater willingness to recognize electoral victories of the PAN than those claimed by the PRD, except in Cárdenas's home state of Michoacán.

Barring a complete opening of the Mexican political system to permit unfettered competition between the PRI and its opposition, the strategic options available to the opposition parties appear limited to three: First, by protesting electoral fraud through mass demonstrations, civil disobedience, and appeals to international public opinion, each opposition party can raise incrementally the cost of fraud to the regime in terms of internal legitimacy and foreign investor confidence, while continuing to run candidates

---

[59]Cuauhtémoc Cárdenas has summarized his party's differences with the Salinas government as follows: "The issue is not whether the economy should be modernized and opened up, nor whether many of the costlier programs of the Mexican welfare state should be made more cost-effective and efficient....The real issue is at what speed, how deeply, and under what conditions these changes should be undertaken...[and] who should pay the unavoidable costs that a program of economic restructuring entails." (Cuauhtémoc Cárdenas, "Misunderstanding Mexico," *Foreign Policy*, Winter, 1989-90, 115.) See also: Miguel Angel Centeno, *Mexico in the 1990s: Government and Opposition Speak Out*, Current Issue Brief No. 1 (La Jolla, Calif.: Center for U.S.-Mexican Studies, University of California, San Diego, 1991).

[60]For example, in México State, which includes much of the Mexico City metropolitan area, the PRD's candidates for state and local office in the 1990 elections polled only one-fifth as many votes as presidential candidate Cuauhtémoc Cárdenas won in 1988.

and to negotiate election results with the government. Second, the opposition parties could attempt to form a national front to insist on clean elections and accelerated democratization. The PRD has already called for a "National Accord for Democracy," embracing all opposition parties and dissident groups within the PRI, to defend the vote in future national elections. Such a national front could not, however, run its own candidates, as the Cardenista coalition did in 1988; the revised electoral law enacted in 1989-90 effectively prevents "fusion" candidacies. Finally, the opposition parties could adopt an abstentionist stance, refusing to participate in the PRI-dominated electoral process and devoting themselves to other forms of confrontation and resistance, public education, and support for social movements. The fact that the opposition parties have such a limited and less-than-attractive set of options is further evidence that Mexico's transition to a well-institutionalized, competitive, multiparty system is far from complete.

POLITICAL REFORM MEASURES

Many times during the last four decades, segments of the Mexican political elite, including most incoming presidents, have called for "reforms" of the system of parties and elections.[61] Some reform projects have focused on the ruling party, especially the need to democratize its internal procedures of governance and candidate selection. Others have concentrated on the relationship between the PRI and the opposition parties, prescribing changes in electoral rules that would expand opportunities for the opposition. The two types of political reform are, of course, interrelated. Reforming the PRI is generally believed to be a necessary, though not sufficient, condition for broader political liberalization in Mexico.

The stimuli for political reform attempts have varied over time. Shocks to the system—the nationwide teachers' and railroad workers' strikes of 1958, the student protest movement and massacre of 1968, and the economic crises of 1975-76 and 1982-88—have prompted efforts by political elites to create new safety valves for opposition activity and accumulated social tensions. Beginning in the mid-1970s, political reform projects were also fueled by the relentless climb of voter abstentionism and the continuing decline in voter support for the PRI. To some concerned members of the political elite, these indicators of rising political

---

[61]For a more detailed review of these various political reform projects, dating back to the Miguel Alemán administration in 1946, see John J. Bailey, *Governing Mexico* (New York: St. Martin's Press, 1988), 106-20. See also Wayne A. Cornelius, "Political Liberalization in an Authoritarian Regime: Mexico, 1976-1985," in *Mexican Politics in Transition*, ed. Judith Gentleman (Boulder, Colo.: Westview Press, 1988), 15-39.

alienation and cynicism suggested that the electoral mechanism itself was being exhausted as a vehicle for legitimating the regime and convincing private investors of its basic stability.

Since 1963 there have been five major revisions of the federal election laws. The thrust of these changes has been to bolster the PRI by giving it a more credible opposition to run against. A limited form of proportional representation was introduced to increase opposition party representation in the federal Congress, and the formation of new political parties was encouraged. The 1977 electoral law reforms made it possible for a party to qualify for legal registration by polling only 1.5 percent of the votes cast in a nationwide election or by enrolling at least 65,000 members. The 1989-90 electoral code revisions ostensibly were aimed at reducing the PRI's advantages over the opposition parties, particularly by making it more difficult for PRI and government officials to commit electoral fraud. Henceforth, all parties will have access to the federal electoral commission's computers when votes are being counted; preliminary election results must be announced the same day, as opposed to waiting a week for the official results; new, nationwide electoral rolls will be compiled, requiring the re-registration of more than 40 million eligible voters; new voting credentials bearing the holder's photograph will be issued to all voters; and the PRI will no longer have majority control over the entity responsible for certifying final election results.

These changes, if fully and impartially implemented, would eliminate some, but not all, of the mechanisms traditionally used by the PRI-government apparatus to rig elections. However, the same revision of the electoral code included a "governability clause," which gives the party winning a plurality of votes, higher than 35 percent, in a national election an automatic majority in the Chamber of Deputies. This provision virtually guarantees continued control of Congress by the PRI, and through it by the president. The end result of these changes is likely to be a more competitive, multiparty system in which the PRI will be the dominant—but no longer hegemonic—party, with no significant diminution of presidential power.

Most attempts to reform the official party have taken the form of efforts to increase grassroots participation in the PRI's candidate selection process (but mainly for municipal presidencies) and to dilute the power of the sectoral leaders—the old-guard party bosses who run the PRI-affiliated labor, campesino, and urban professional and slum-dweller ("popular" sector) organizations. Traditionally, the lists of PRI nominees for congressional seats and many other public offices have been the result of secret negotiations between the president and national-level sectoral leaders. The candidate selections reflected the relative power of each of the three sectors within the ruling party.[62] Under new party statutes approved at the PRI's fourteenth national assembly in September 1990, citizens will be encouraged to affiliate with the PRI as individuals, without having to belong to one of the sectoral organizations. Moreover, in the future, relatively fewer of the PRI's candidates will be designated by the sectoral organizations. The party's territorially defined structures (local and state committees) will have a greater voice in candidate selection and other areas of decision making. The collapse of the PRI's "sectoral vote" in recent elections has given considerable impetus to these changes. They also reflect President Salinas's strong conviction that territoriality—especially residence in an urban neighborhood—has become the key basis for political mobilization in a country where most people live in large cities, do not belong to labor unions, and increasingly participate in locally oriented social movements that have emerged outside of the PRI's sectoral structures.[63]

While the new rules will reduce the discretionary power of PRI and government functionaries, there is no guarantee that they will translate into fundamentally different behavior in future elections. Previous reforms did nothing to ensure respect for election results by PRI operatives, especially at the local and state levels. Ultimately, the holding of fair and clean elections still depends on the will of the president and other senior officials, as well as their ability to secure the cooperation of lower-echelon PRI leaders. Would-be reformers within the PRI-government apparatus continue to encounter strong resistance from the so-called dinosaurs entrenched in the sectoral organizations (especially the *oficialista* labor movement) and state and local PRI machines. These old-guard PRIista leaders have nothing to gain and a great deal to lose personally from a more rapid political opening with genuine contestation of elections at all levels. President Salinas has adopted a low-risk, gradualist approach to political reform, to prevent open

---

[62]For example, in 1988, 18 percent of the PRI's nominations for congressional seats went to representatives of the party's campesino sector, 22 percent to the labor sector, and 60 percent to the "popular" sector. The campesino sector, which until 1964 had received half of the PRI's congressional nominations, has lost ground continuously to the labor and popular sectors.

[63]See Cornelius, Gentleman, and Smith, eds., *Mexico's Alternative Political Futures*, 26-36.

ruptures within the PRI that might threaten the completion of his government's economic restructuring program.[64]

---

[64]Salinas explained his position as follows: "When you are introducing such a strong economic reform, you must make sure that you build the [necessary] political consensus around it. If you are simultaneously introducing additional drastic political reform, you may end up with no reform at all. And we want to have reform, not a disintegrated country" (quoted in Nathan Gardels, "North America Free Trade: Mexico's Route to Upward Mobility," *New Perspectives Quarterly* 8:1 [Winter 1991]: 8).

Campesinos, Organized Labor, and the Military: Pillars of the Regime?

The Mexican state's relationships with three major sectors of society—campesinos (peasants), organized labor, and the military—have been central to the stability of the regime since the 1930s. Indeed, they are often referred to as "pillars of the regime," in recognition of their crucial role in maintaining the political system. In this section we will sketch the basic terms of the relationships between Mexico's ruling elite and these three sectors, and identify some current sources of tension that might disrupt them.

STATE-CAMPESINO RELATIONS

From 1810 until 1929, the Mexican peasantry was among the most rebellious in Latin America, engaging in frequent armed uprising against both local and national elites.[65] After 1930, however, the rural poor became the largest support group of the Mexican government and of the official party. As a rule, this was the one segment of society that could always be counted upon to vote for PRI candidates and to participate in electoral rallies and in public demonstrations supporting government policies. Perhaps more than any other segment of society, the low-income rural population believed in the ideals of the Mexican Revolution and in the government's intention to realize those ideals.

The campesino sector includes three important subgroups: landless wage laborers (*jornaleros*), beneficiaries of land reform (*ejidatarios*), and owners of very small properties (*minifundistas*). Their support has been secured by two principal means: government policies that distribute vital resources (land, water, credit, fertilizer, etc.) to the rural population, and mechanisms of political control in the countryside.

[65]See Friedrich Katz, ed., *Riot, Rebellion, and Revolution: Rural Social Conflict in Mexico* (Princeton, N.J.: Princeton University Press, 1988).

Traditionally, land has been the most important resource sought by campesinos, and land reform the most consistent government promise to them. Lázaro Cárdenas distributed more land more rapidly than any president before or since. In so doing, he secured campesino support for his policies in other areas, while extending the network of government-affiliated organizations whose members were actual or aspiring ejidatarios. The establishment of a nationwide confederation of campesino organizations, the CNC, and its incorporation into the official party in 1938 institutionalized the relationship between the state and those campesinos who had received land under the agrarian reform program. (Other sectors of the campesino population—landless wage laborers and very small private landholders—were not included in the CNC.) Thenceforth, CNC officials would serve as intermediaries in most transactions between ejidatarios and the government ministries and banks that dispensed resources to the ejidos. The CNC has also been the organization through which the campesino sector endorses PRI candidates for public office and participates in electoral campaigns and other regime-supported political acitvities.

The CNC's organizational dominance in the countryside has been contested increasingly by dissident groups. Three sets of grievances have fueled independent campesino organizations: unmet demands for land, especially in regions where large, undivided landholdings in excess of the legal size limit persist despite the existence of groups petitioning for land redistribution; complaints about low crop prices, limited access to markets, and inequitable distribution of agricultural inputs like water and credit by government agencies; and wage and employment problems affecting landless agricultural laborers. In addition, political grievances—usually rooted in the economic problems just mentioned— against caciques and municipal authorities have provoked campesino occupations of local government offices.

Despite the inroads made by autonomous movements since the late 1970s, most *organized* peasants in Mexico today are still members of CNC-affiliated organizations. However, the CNC's grip on the peasantry is increasingly tenuous, as demonstrated by the 1988 election. While Salinas's margin of victory came from the country's most rural electoral districts, analysis of the election results shows that the PRI had its greatest difficulties in those districts where the party's congressional candidate was affiliated with the CNC (as opposed to the labor or popular sector) *and* where the Cardenista front had a presence.[66] This suggests that

---

[66]Pacheco Méndez, "Estructura y resultados electorales," 20.

when provided with an alternative to the PRI and the economic policies now associated with it, many campesinos will readily abandon their traditional allegiance to the official party.

The CNC's dilemma is partly of its own making. The CNC leadership has become increasingly divorced from the federation's social base. For many years, peasants have been manipulated, intimidated, and swindled by CNC leaders as well as by representatives of government agencies responsible for rural development programs.[67] Moreover, officials have often forged pernicious alliances with the caciques who control many ejido communities. These local bosses have amassed power and wealth by selling or renting ejido land to private farmers, with the acquiescence or active connivance of government officials. The CNC has become completely compromised by these transactions.

Rural support for the regime has also been undermined by major shifts in government policies affecting campesino interests. Each of Mexico's last three presidents has publicly declared that the land redistribution program, begun in 1917, has ended because allegedly there are no more large landholdings to be expropriated. The main function of the Agrarian Reform Ministry has changed from processing peasants' petitions for land to granting certificates of "nonaffectability" to cattle ranchers and other private landowners whose holdings exceed the legal limits, thereby protecting them from expropriation.[68] Government policy in recent sexenios has emphasized the need to boost agricultural production by reorganizing the small ejido plots doled out through the agrarian reform program into larger, supposedly more efficient units of production—not to create additional small peasant producers.

The efficacy of clientelistic PRI controls over the peasantry also declined sharply during the economic crisis of the 1980s, as the government resources available for meeting the basic needs of landed campesinos contracted. Public spending on rural infrastructure, agricultural credit, and crop price supports declined drastically, even while other government policies were driving up the prices of fuel, fertilizer, and other necessary agricultural inputs. Government policy toward the rural sector now emphasizes linking "middle peasants" (farmers whose operations could become commercially viable with minimal government assistance—

---

[67]For examples, see Merilee S. Grindle, *Bureaucrats, Peasants, and Politicians in Mexico: A Case Study in Public Policy* (Berkeley: University of California Press, 1977), 147-63.

[68]Nevertheless, the hunger for land persists. Official statistics show that by the end of 1986 more than 43 percent of the economically active population in rural areas—some 3.2 million persons—were landless (Harvey, *The New Agrarian Movement in Mexico*, 7).

about 18 percent of all landholders) with domestic and international agribusinesses that can provide them with financing, technology, and marketing opportunities. For the subsistence farmers (80 percent of the total) who are too poor to meet that criterion, there are limited social welfare programs like PRONASOL. Clearly the era of massive government subsidy programs aimed at small-scale peasant agriculture—programs initiated in the early 1970s and vastly expanded during the oil boom years of 1980-82—has ended. Adjusting to these new realities, more and more residents of Mexico's rural communities are abandoning agricultural production altogether and turning to wage labor (often in the United States) as their primary source of income.

Unless the CNC can expand the range of issues on which it can "deliver" beyond its traditional focus on land tenure, the PRI and the government may find their capacity for mobilization in the countryside permanently diminished. Despite its need to retain a "safe" rural electoral base, it is not at all clear what benefits a technocratic regime committed to fiscal discipline and letting market forces work will be able to offer the small farmer—much less Mexico's large population of landless rural workers—in the foreseeable future.

THE STATE AND ORGANIZED LABOR

Since 1940, the Mexican government's control over organized labor has been essential to the strategy of economic development that the state has pursued. By tightly regulating the formation of new unions, wage increases, strike activity, and even the resolution of individual worker grievances against employers, the government has been able to guarantee a disciplined and relatively cheap labor force, attractive to both foreign and domestic investors. Government control over labor strikes has been especially tight and has grown progressively tighter over time. During the 1938-45 period, an average of 32 percent of all workers' petitions for strikes were authorized (recognized as legal strikes) by the federal government; only 2 percent of all strike petitions were approved during the 1963-88 period. Between 1982 and 1988, despite high inflation and severe unemployment problems, the level of strike activity actually declined.[69]

---

[69]Kevin J. Middlebrook, *Organized Labor and the State in Postrevolutionary Mexico* (forthcoming), chap. 5. See also Alberto Aziz Nassif, *El estado mexicano y la CTM* (México, D.F.: La Casa Chata, 1989); and Kevin J. Middlebrook, ed., *Unions, Workers, and the State in Mexico* (La Jolla, Calif.: Center for U.S.-Mexican Studies, University of California, San Diego, 1991).

Wage levels for most unionized workers are determined through behind-the-scenes negotiations between national-level labor leaders and senior government officials—not between labor and management. The outcomes of these talks are ceilings on wage increases, which become negotiating guidelines for lower-level union officials throughout the country. Since 1983, the Confederation of Mexican Workers (CTM)—Mexico's largest and most politically influential labor organization—has been an active and essential partner in the government's economic stabilization program, settling for wage increases significantly below the rate of inflation. Since 1987, the CTM leadership has signed a series of "economic solidarity pacts" with the government and the business community which have kept wages under tight control, even while allowing many prices to rise. Unlike virtually all other labor federations in Latin America during the last ten years, the CTM has not opposed the government's policy of privatizing state-owned enterprises (often resulting in significant job losses) or other "neoliberal" policies intended to restructure the country's economy along free market lines.

The largely captive labor movement has also helped the government to maintain political control by keeping lower-class demand making fragmented. From 1955 to about 1975, through a steady stream of government-orchestrated wage increases and expansions of nonwage benefits (subsidized food, clothing, housing, health care, transportation, etc.), the government created a privileged elite of unionized workers within the urban working class. These nonwage benefits served as a cushion during the economic crisis of the 1980s, partially insulating unionized workers from the ravages of high inflation and government austerity measures.

Of the three main sectors of the PRI, it has been the labor sector, dominated by the CTM and Fidel Velázquez, the undisputed leader of the government-affiliated labor movement since 1949, that has been the strongest and best organized for collective political action. Unionized workers could be mobilized quickly and on a national scale for mass demonstrations to support government policies, campaign rallies, and voter registration drives. Organized labor's representatives—especially the members of the national teachers' union—have also been very important to the PRI in mobilizing its vote in rural areas and small towns.

From the government's viewpoint, the high degree of continuity in CTM leadership has also been an important advantage. Although several of the eight presidents under whom Fidel Velázquez has served have had major policy disagreements with him, there is no question that his long reign and political dexterity have contributed greatly to the stability of the Mexican political system. By the same reasoning, Velázquez's death (he was born in 1900) could release centrifugal forces within the labor movement that could complicate at least temporarily the government's relations with organized labor, since Velázquez's successor is unlikely to be as slavishly supportive of the regime and its policies as he has been. Over the past ten years, Velázquez has repeatedly backed down from threats to call a general strike if the government failed to grant wage increases of the magnitude sought by the CTM. In every instance, organized labor has settled for less—usually much less.

Unable to secure significant concessions from the government on the wage front, the CTM has shifted its emphasis from wage increases to employment protection and safeguarding workers' purchasing power through the creation of union-owned retail stores, consumer cooperatives, and other "social sector" enterprises. Until 1991, the CTM also sought, and received, modest increases in political patronage. For example, the share of congressional seats allocated by the PRI leadership to the labor sector rose from 14 percent in 1976 to 22 percent in 1988. Although expanded political patronage is of limited benefit to rank-and-file union members, it has helped to maintain the support of the CTM leadership for government policies.

One of the paradoxes of organized labor is that, while professing to be the staunchest guardian of Mexico's revolutionary heritage, it has become the most conservative sector of the ruling coalition in recent years. The CTM hierarchy has advocated repression of most forms of political dissent and resisted any changes in the rules of electoral competition that would benefit opposition forces. Moreover, the labor sector has continued its practice of nominating notoriously corrupt, old-style political "dinosaurs" as candidates for many of the elective offices allocated to it. The confederation's leaders apparently fear that the reformist impulse might spread beyond the electoral system to the oficialista labor movement itself, strengthening pressures for greater intraunion democracy. This conceivably could threaten the jobs of many entrenched labor leaders.

CTM-affiliated unions have been run like old-fashioned political machines, with the leaders, who had to be reelected periodically, trading material benefits for votes. As the material payoffs to the rank and file have diminished, oficialista labor leaders have lost credibility and legitimacy in the eyes of their members and resorted to heavy-handed authoritarian tactics in order to keep control. New entrants to the labor force are much better educated and less willing to accept autocratic, corrupt, often ganster-like leadership by union bosses than were preceding generations. In recent years, the government has found it necessary to use police more frequently to break up unauthorized strikes and repress challenges to incumbent union leaders by dissident unionists.

Independent unionism gained a small foothold in the labor movement during the 1970s, mainly among university faculty and staff employees, and workers in the automobile, mining, electrical, telephone, and nuclear energy industries. Technological changes and deteriorating working conditions in these industries had created new worker grievances that were being ignored by established union organizations.[70] In 1979, a dissident movement emerged within the national teachers' union, and by 1989 it had gained enough support to stage a nationwide strike by a half million teachers. This gave President Carlos Salinas a sufficient pretext to force the resignation of the union's long-entrenched president, Carlos Jonguitud Barrios.

Despite its sporadic triumphs, independent unionism has not progressed very far in Mexico. Widely detested union caciques like Jonguitud and Joaquín Hernández Galicia ("La Quina"), the head of the oil workers' union, also deposed by Salinas in 1989, have been replaced by leaders handpicked by the president who are less autocratic but more servile to presidential will than their predecessors. Independent unions have not won the ability to organize national-level unions that could compete against the large, nationally organized, CTM-affiliated unions for the support of the working classes; thus, the most militant independent union movements have remained localized and isolated. With few exceptions, the government has been able to neutralize efforts by the Cardenista opposition to foment independent union militancy. It provides economic subsidies and political protection to its allies within the labor movement, while using its regulatory controls over union registration and strike activity to discipline potential opponents and create divisions within dissident movements.

As signaled by the 1988 elections, when millions of CTM-affiliated union members abandoned the PRI's candidates, organized labor's utility to the regime as an instrument of voter mobilization and political control will continue to decline. Recognizing this, the government sharply reduced the share of candidates backed by the CTM among the PRI's nominees for congressional seats in the

---

[70]For a case study, see Kevin J. Middlebrook, "Union Democratization in the Mexican Automobile Industry," *Latin American Research Review* 24:2 (1989): 69-93.

1991-94 term. However, as Mexico's economy is restructured and the nation's development strategy becomes increasingly dependent on export performance, the oficialista labor movement will become more important than ever as a pillar of support for the government's macroeconomic policies. Maintaining Mexico's comparative advantage in world markets (mainly owing to low wage scales), eliminating rigidities and inefficiencies that constrain productivity, privatizing or shutting down additional money-losing state-owned enterprises, preventing a resurgence of inflation—all will require continuing concessions from organized labor. In return, the ruling technocrats will continue to defer to the political preferences and sensibilities of oficialista labor leaders, including their fear of a rapid transition to democracy.

THE MILITARY IN POLITICS

By the end of the Cárdenas era, Mexico had a largely demilitarized political system: political activity by high-ranking military men had been confined to nonviolent competition and bargaining within an institutionalized decision-making framework that was clearly dominated by civilian elites.

Beginning with Calles in the 1920s, Mexican presidents used three basic tools to achieve military disengagement from politics: frequent rotation of military zone commanders (to prevent them from building up large personal followings of troops and local politicians); generous material incentives for staying out of politics; and a policy of requiring military men who wanted to remain politically active to do so essentially as private individuals rather than as representatives of the military as an institution. Thus, the "military sector" of the official party was dissolved by President Avila Camacho soon after he took office in 1940; and the military bloc of representatives in the Congress was dissolved in the following year. The members of these military sectors were encouraged to affiliate themselves with one of the other sectors of the PRI; most were absorbed by the "popular" sector.

Since the 1940s the number of military men serving in high-level nonmilitary public offices has steadily declined. Up to 1964 it was traditional for the president to appoint a military man to serve in the post of PRI chairman; since then, that post has been held only by career politicians. Typically, the only cabinet posts now held by active military officers are secretary of national defense and secretary of the navy.[71] State governorships held by career military officers dropped from fifteen (out of thirty-one) during the Alemán administration to one or two during the Echeverría, López Portillo, and de la Madrid sexenios and none under Salinas. During the 1988-91 congressional term, military officers held three of the sixty-four Senate seats and four out of five hundred seats in the Chamber of Deputies.

The most striking indicator of the military's decline as a political institution is its share of total government expenditures, which dropped from 17 percent in 1940 to 5-6 percent in the 1970s and to 1-3 percent in the 1980s. As a percentage of gross domestic product, Mexico's military expenditures averaged less than 1 percent during the 1960-84 period—the lowest of any Latin American country, including Costa Rica, which has only a national police force. Spending on the military has increased moderately in recent years, partly in response to U.S. pressure on the Mexican government to step up its drug eradication and interdiction efforts. By 1990 Mexico had about 140,000 men under arms, over 25 percent of whom were engaged full-time in the antidrug campaign.[72]

While the Mexican military is relatively small and impoverished in terms of military hardware, successive governments have taken care to provide a steady flow of material benefits for military personnel. They have received regular salary increases (even during the worst years of economic crisis and government austerity budgets) and a variety of generous nonwage benefits (housing, medical care, loans, subsidized consumer goods) which added about 40 percent to base pay.

Despite the long-term decline in its influence on government policy making, the Mexican military retains a capacity to influence important political events. Civilian presidents still call on the military for support in crisis situations. In recent sexenios such support has taken the form of armed repression of dissident groups (as in the 1968 massacre of student demonstrators in Mexico City and the 1990 ejection of Cardenista militants from sixteen town halls in Michoacán, which they had occupied to protest electoral fraud); highly effective counterinsurgency campaigns against rural guerrillas during the 1960s and 1970s; the breaking of major, unauthorized labor strikes (such as a strike at Cananea, the country's largest mine, in 1989); and the arrest of major political figures accused of criminal offenses (e.g., "La Quina," head of the oil workers'

---

[71]Carlos Salinas's Gobernación minister, Fernando Gutiérrez Barrios, is the first graduate of the national military college to hold a nonmilitary cabinet post since the Díaz Ordaz (1964-70) administration (Camp, "Camarillas in Mexican Politics," 104).

[72]See Roderic A. Camp, *Generals in the Palacio: The Military in Modern Mexico* (New York: Oxford University Press, forthcoming 1992).

union). As the Echeverría and López Portillo sexenios drew to a close amid fiscal chaos and erratic presidential behavior, rumors were widespread that the military would seize control of the government. In both cases, top-ranking military officers helped to bring an end to the rumor campaign and to guarantee a nonviolent transfer of power to a new civilian president, by publicly reaffirming their loyalty to the nation's institutional order.

Since 1985, civilian authorities have called on the military to provide highly visible "security" for elections. Formerly, troops were deployed only in response to election-related disturbances if they occurred. Now they can be seen before, during, and after the elections, particularly in states that are strongholds of the opposition parties. The opposition charges that the huge military presence in these places is intended to intimidate their supporters from going to the polls and from taking to the streets to protest fraudulent election practices.

The routinized use of the military for such political control purposes could strain civil-military relations. "The military doesn't like to perform police functions," explained one general.[73] The military's public image was badly tarnished by its role in the 1968 student massacre, and senior officers are loathe to become involved in any situation that poses similar risks. In recent years, the military establishment has also become increasingly concerned by drug-related corruption in its ranks. As the military's role in the government's antidrug campaign has increased, so have allegations that military zone commanders and even the secretaries of defense and the navy have been involved in drug trafficking and protection schemes.

Because the military is an important pillar of the regime, any decline in its previously strong support for civilian authorities could be destabilizing. Recognizing this, each new president has reaffirmed the long-standing policy of honoring the military effusively in public rhetoric, respecting its autonomy in promotions and other matters of internal governance, and maintaining the flow of material rewards to military personnel. Recent presidents have also supported a major upgrading of military education. By 1985, the military education system included a new National Defense College, conferring a master's degree in national security and defense management, and twenty-two other schools that offered training in a wide range of professions and technical skills.

This expansion of educational opportunities has "increased the military's capacity to take on new political functions should

---

[73]General Luis Garfías, remarks at a research workshop on the Mexican military, Center for U.S.-Mexican Studies, University of California, San Diego, March 1984.

Mexico suddenly experience a crisis of governability or if civil-military relations deteriorated beyond a certain point."[74] Most observers, however, do not anticipate the reemergence of the military as an independent political actor *unless* the country's civilian rulers fail completely to maintain law and order. An extremely widespread, totally uncontrolled mass mobilization—whatever its origins—might well provoke a military intervention, probably aimed at restoring order rather than installing a military government. Some specialists on the Mexican military doubt that it has the capacity to seize power in such a situation, even if senior officers wished to. Others argue that whether or not the military believes itself capable of ruling, it might opt to take power if it perceives a generalized threat of social turmoil and institutional breakdown. Most scholars agree that it is the malfunctioning of civilian authority—rather than the military's own ambitions—that would be most likely to cause the military to assume an overt political role once again.[75]

---

[74]José Luis Piñeyro, "The Modernization of the Mexican Armed Forces," in *Democracy under Siege: New Military Power in Latin America*, ed. Augusto Varas (Westport, Conn.: Greenwood, 1989), 116.

[75]See David Ronfeldt, ed., *The Modern Mexican Military: A Reassessment*, Monograph Series, no. 15 (La Jolla, Calif.: Center for U.S.-Mexican Studies, University of California, San Diego, 1984); and Roderic A. Camp, "Civilian Supremacy in Mexico: The Case of a Post-revolutionary Military," in *Military Intervention and Withdrawal*, ed. Constantine P. Danopoulos (London: Routledge, 1990).

Political Culture and Socialization

Most of what we know about Mexican political culture is based on research completed during the period of sustained economic growth and virtually unchallenged one-party rule in Mexico, from 1940 to the mid-1970s. There is now some sample survey-based research on mass political culture in the 1980s, but not yet enough to confidently document the changes in core values, attitudes, and behaviors that most observers assume have occurred during more than fifteen years of economic crises and government austerity.

The portrait of Mexican political culture that emerges from studies of previous decades can be summarized as follows:[76] Mexicans are highly supportive of the political institutions that evolved from the Mexican Revolution, and they endorse the democratic principles embodied in the Constitution of 1917. However, they are critical of government performance, especially in creating jobs, reducing social and economic inequality, and delivering basic public services. Most government bureaucrats and politicians are viewed as distant, elitist, and self-serving, if not corrupt. Mexicans are deeply cynical about the electoral process and pessimistic about their ability to affect election outcomes. The average Mexican regards participation in electoral campaigns, attendance at rallies, voting, and affiliation with political parties as ritualistic activities. While engaging in such activities may be necessary to extract benefits from the system, individual citizens are believed to have little effect on the shape of public policy or the selection of public officials. Mexicans prefer individual rather than collective strategies for solving problems. Their contacts with government

---

[76]For a critical review of this literature, see Ann L. Craig and Wayne A. Cornelius, "Political Culture in Mexico: Continuities and Revisionist Interpretations," in *The Civic Culture Revisited*, ed. Gabriel Almond and Sidney Verba (Newbury Park, Calif.: Sage, 1989).

agencies typically have been brokered through networks of politically connected intermediaries, including local caciques, although new social movements are insisting on greater autonomy from such brokers.

On the surface, this combination of attitudes and beliefs seems to be internally contradictory. How could Mexicans support a political system that they see as unresponsive or capricious at best? Historically, popular support for the Mexican political system has derived from three sources: the revolutionary origins of the regime, the government's role in promoting economic growth, and its performance in distributing concrete, material benefits to a substantial proportion of the Mexican population since the Cárdenas era. Each of these traditional sources of support has been undermined to some extent in the last decade.

The official interpretation of the 1910 Revolution stresses symbols (or myths) such as social justice, democracy, the need for national unity, and the popular origins of the current regime. The government's identification with these symbols has been reinforced constantly by the mass media, public schools, and the mass organizations affiliated with the official party. Over the years, the party's electoral appeals were explicitly designed to link its candidates with agrarian reform and other revered ideals of the Revolution, with national heroes like Emiliano Zapata and Lázaro Cárdenas, and with the national flag (the PRI emblem conveniently has the same colors, in the same arrangement). Beginning in 1987, the neo-Cardenista opposition mounted the first serious challenge to the PRI and government's claim to the revolutionary mantle.

Relatively few Mexicans have based their support for the system primarily upon its revolutionary origins or symbolic outputs, however. For many sectors of the population, symbols were supplemented with particularistic material rewards: plots of land or titles to land that had been occupied illegally, schools, low-cost medical care, agricultural crop price supports, government-subsidized food and other consumer goods, and public-sector jobs. For more than forty years, the personal receipt of some material "favor" from the official party-government apparatus, or the hope that such benefits might be received in the future, ensured fairly high levels of mass support for the system.

Despite their keen dissatisfaction with the government's recent economic performance, electoral corruption, and other irritations, the vast majority of Mexicans remain "system loyalists." Survey data collected during the 1980s demonstrated consistently the Mexican people's fundamental aversion to concepts of radical transformation, especially those promoted by the Marxist left.[77] A Gallup poll conducted in May 1988 showed that 61 percent of Mexicans thought that an opposition party victory at the national level would not enhance the country's economic prospects, and over half believed that an opposition victory would touch off social disorder.[78] In short, public opinion surveys in the late 1980s portrayed a citizenry still tethered to its traditional political moorings.

Nevertheless, Mexicans are increasingly willing to criticize the way in which the system often functions. Surveys show that Mexicans at all income levels are concerned about "bad government." Their assessments of politics, politicians, government bureaucrats, and the police are predominantly cynical and mistrustful.[79] Corruption is assumed to be pervasive, but historically most Mexicans have tolerated it, within limits, as a price to be paid in order to extract benefits from the system.[80] Such tolerance may be declining, however. During the last ten years, corruption in the PRI-government apparatus has been one of the most successful campaign issues for the opposition parties, especially the PAN.

Mexicans increasingly blame their economic distress on failures of government performance. In previous decades, the government received much credit for stimulating and guiding the nation's economic development. The economic slowdowns, inflationary spirals, and currency devaluations of the 1970s and 1980s wiped out those positive perceptions. Particularly among middle-class Mexicans, many of whom saw their personal assets and living standards decline precipitously during the 1980s, loss of confidence in the government's ability to manage the economy was dramatic. Even among urban industrial workers, there is evidence of much dissatisfaction with the economic policies of

---

[77]The data supporting this generalization are summarized in John J. Bailey, "Reform of the Mexican Political System: Prospects for Change in 1987-1988" (paper prepared for the Office of External Research, U.S. Department of State, July 1987).

[78]Dan Williams, "Polls Becoming an Issue in Mexico's Campaign," *Los Angeles Times*, June 28, 1988.

[79]A recent national survey found that the most trusted social institutions in Mexico were the schools and the Catholic church; the least trusted were the legislature, bureaucrats, and elected public officials. See Alberto Hernández Medina and Luis Navarro Rodríguez, eds., *Cómo somos los mexicanos* (Mexico City: Centro de Estudios Educativos, 1987), 22.

[80]In a 1979 survey of Mexico City residents, 90 percent agreed with the following statement: "If you really want something from the government, you can almost always get it with a bribe" (Lee Dye, "What Mexicans Think: Their Trust Is in Themselves," *Los Angeles Times*, special supplement on Mexico, July 15, 1979).

recent Mexican administrations and increasingly negative attitudes toward general features of the political system.[81]

The Mexican public's negativism toward the political process is reflected in attitudes toward political parties in general. A Gallup poll taken in July 1987 revealed that 38 percent of a national sample of Mexicans had no party preference. In another national survey, conducted in April 1990, nearly 51 percent of the respondents indicated that they did not support any political party.[82] These and other survey results suggest a sullen, cynical electorate, in which generalized "antiparty" attitudes are increasingly prevalent.

Moreover, all parties—including the PRI—have vague and confused images. As a result, Mexicans are more likely to identify with strong personalities like Cuauhtémoc Cárdenas and Carlos Salinas than with the political parties led by these figures. The lack of deeply rooted partisan attachments was demonstrated clearly in the 1988 election, when many of those who voted for the Cardenista front were found to be ex-PAN supporters who had originally been PRI voters! These floating protest voters were not ideologically committed to the left any more than they had been to the rightist opposition or the PRI in previous elections. Similarly, in the 1989 gubernatorial election in Baja California Norte, much of the support for victorious PANista candidate Ernesto Ruffo came from persons who had voted for Cuauhtémoc Cárdenas in the 1988 presidential election.

MASS POLITICAL SOCIALIZATION

How do Mexicans form their attitudes toward the political system? In addition to the family, the schools and the Catholic church are important sources of preadult political learning. All schools, including church-affiliated and lay private schools, must follow a government-approved curriculum and use the same set of free textbooks, written by the federal Ministry of Education. Although the private schools' compliance with the official curriculum is often nominal, control over the content of textbooks gives the government an instrument for socializing children to a formal set of political values. This learning supports the regime and stresses revolutionary symbols. Its impact is reflected in the beliefs of Mexican schoolchildren that their country has experienced a true

---

[81]Charles L. Davis, *Working-Class Mobilization and Political Control: Venezuela and Mexico* (Louisville: University Press of Kentucky, 1989).

[82]Data provided by the Centro de Estudios de Opinión Pública, S.C., Mexico City.

social revolution; that although this revolution is still incomplete, the government is working diligently to realize its goals; and that the president is an omnipotent authority figure, whose principal function is to "maintain order in the country."[83]

The Catholic church is another key source of values that affect political behavior in Mexico. Private, church-run schools have proliferated in recent years, and along with secular private schools, they provide education for a large portion of children from middle- and upper-class families. Religious schools and priests preach against socialism, criticize anticlerical laws and policies, and promote individual initiative (as opposed to governmental action). They also stress the need for moral Christian behavior, which is seen as absent in the corrupt, self-serving, materialistic world of politics.

As adults, Mexicans learn about politics from their personal encounters with PRI and government functionaries and by participating in organizations, such as community improvement associations, that petition the government for collective benefits. Research shows that in Mexico, attitudes such as political efficacy (a sense of competence to influence the political process), cynicism about politicians, and evaluations of government performance in delivering goods and services are strongly influenced by political learning that occurs after childhood and adolescence. The campesino who has been involved in years of inconclusive efforts to secure an all-weather road for his village is more likely to be aware of the inefficiency, corruption, and arbitrary interpretation of rules that characterize much of the Mexican public bureaucracy. Conversely, the resident of an urban squatter settlement who has participated in a well-organized movement that secured land titles for settlement residents is more likely to feel competent to influence government decisions, at least as part of an organized group.

Mexicans have been taught two sets of political values that increasingly seem to be in conflict:[84] On the one hand, mainly through the schools, they are formally taught a normative set of values about revolutionary institutions and objectives that identify the general public interest with the political system. On the other hand, adult experiences teach them how Mexican politics "really work." The PAN, and now the PRD, have sought to capitalize on the perceived gap between democratic-constitutional

---

[83]Rafael Segovia, *La politización del niño mexicano* (Mexico City: El Colegio de México, 1975), 51-58.

[84]For a fuller explication of this point, see Kenneth M. Coleman and Charles L. Davis, *Politics and Culture in Mexico* (Ann Arbor: Institute for Social Research, University of Michigan, 1988).

values and "real" politics. Support for the PRI has been declining among the better-educated population. Education has increased criticism of the electoral system and reduced tolerance for human rights violations by the government and security forces. Higher levels of education are also associated with higher support for the right to dissent and other democratic liberties.[85]

POLITICAL PARTICIPATION

Most political participation in Mexico has been of two broad types: ritualistic, regime-supportive activities (e.g., voting, attending campaign rallies), and petitioning or contacting of public officials to influence the allocation of some public good or service. Voting in national elections has been the most widespread form of participation. Until elections were strongly contested in the 1980s, Mexicans typically viewed them and electoral campaigns as purely symbolic events. They knew that they went to the polls not to select those who would govern but to ratify the choice of candidates made earlier by the PRI-government hierarchy. Some voted because they regarded it as their civic duty; others because they wished to avoid difficulty in future dealings with government agencies.[86] Some voted in response to pressures from local caciques, labor union representatives, or other agents of the regime. Despite these concerns, growing numbers of Mexicans have declined to participate in the ritual legitimation of the PRI's hold on public office. Even when elections became moments of genuine political confrontation in many parts of the country, the long-term trend toward lower voter participation persisted.

Mexicans participate in PRI campaign rallies and inaugurations of public works primarily because participation in such government-sanctioned activities can have specific material payoffs. Many of the participants in these events are mobilized by local political leaders who "deliver" *acarreados* ("carted-in" participants), often using government-provided vehicles. The acarreados may receive chits redeemable for a free meal, tickets for a raffle, or simply free transportation to another town for the day. Others participate in such regime-supportive activities because they fear that failure to participate would have personal economic costs. Union members may be penalized a day's pay; some workers

---

[85]John Booth and Mitchell Seligson, "The Political Culture of Authoritarianism in Mexico: A Reexamination," *Latin American Research Review* 19 (1984): 106-24; and Joseph L. Klesner, "Changing Patterns of Electoral Participation and Official Party Support in Mexico," in *Mexican Politics in Transition*, ed. Judith Gentleman, 95-127.
[86]By law, voting is obligatory in Mexico, and evidence of having voted in the most recent election is sometimes required to receive public services.

might even lose their jobs. Title to a plot of land or some keenly sought community benefit like a piped water system might be jeopardized.[87]

Such calculations link the two basic modes of citizen participation in Mexico. For most Mexicans, the reasons for engaging in nonelectoral forms of political activity are highly instrumental and particularistic: participants are usually bent on obtaining specific benefits from the government for themselves, their families, or their community or neighborhood. Participation strategies become ways of manipulating public agencies or officials more effectively on behalf of the individual or group of petitioners—or, increasingly, of protesting failure to benefit or be heard. Nonconfrontational styles of demand making have been the norm, because the government rarely rewards aggressive tactics.

The average Mexican harbors no illusions about the citizen's ability to influence the *content* of public policy or the ordering of government priorities. That kind of influence is exerted only by factions within the political-administrative elite itself and by the most powerful of the organized interest groups to which these factions respond (e.g., national and foreign entrepreneurs, organized labor, the military, and the church). Thus, the average citizen who seeks to influence public policy usually does so during the implementation stage, particularly at the local level. The goal is to obtain preferential application of specific policies or programs. The only governmental actions that can be influenced are low-level decisions on allocation of resources—who will get what under a specific policy.

---

[87]See Wayne A. Cornelius, *Politics and the Migrant Poor in Mexico City* (Stanford, Calif.: Stanford University Press, 1975), 158-60.

Government Performance

ECONOMIC GROWTH AND INEQUALITY

There is little debate about the importance of the state's contribution to the economic development of Mexico since 1940. Massive public investments in infrastructure (roads, dams, telecommunications, electrification) and generous, cheap credit provided to the private sector by Nacional Financiera and other government development banks made possible a high rate of capital accumulation, stimulated high levels of investment by domestic entrepreneurs and foreign corporations, and enabled Mexico to develop a diversified production capacity second only within Latin America to that of Brazil.

From 1940 until well into the 1970s, a strong elite consensus prevailed on the state's role in the economy. The state facilitated private capital accumulation and protected the capitalist system by limiting popular demands for consumption and redistribution of wealth; it established the rules for development; and it participated in the development process as the nation's largest single entrepreneur, employer, and source of investment capital. The state served as "rector" of this "mixed economy," setting broad priorities and channeling investment (both public and private) into strategic sectors. Acting through joint ventures between private firms and state-owned enterprises, the government provided resources for development projects so large that they would have been difficult or impossible to finance from internal (within-the-firm) sources or through borrowing from private banks.

From the mid-1950s to the mid-1970s, the result was the much-touted "Mexican miracle" of sustained economic growth at annual rates of 6-7 percent, coupled with low inflation (5 percent per annum, in the 1955-72 period). By 1980 the gross national product had reached $2,130 per capita, placing Mexico toward the upper end of the World Bank's list of semi-industrialized or "middle-developed" countries. As proprietor of PEMEX, the state oil monopoly, the government was exclusively responsible for developing the crucial oil and natural gas sector of the economy, which by the end of the "oil boom" (1978-81) was generating more than $15 billion a year in export revenues and fueling economic growth of more than 8 percent per year—one of the world's highest growth rates.

It is the *distributive* consequences of this impressive performance in economic development and, since the 1970s, the manner in which it was *financed* by the government that have drawn most of the criticism. From Miguel Alemán (1946-52) to the present, all but one or two of Mexico's presidents and their administrations reflected the private sector's contention that Mexico must first create wealth, and then worry about redistributing it; otherwise, the state would quickly be overwhelmed by popular demands that it could not satisfy. By the early 1970s, however, there was growing evidence that an excessively large portion of Mexico's population had been left behind in the drive for rapid industrialization.

Some benefits of the development process *did* trickle down to the poor. From 1940 to 1980, poverty in absolute terms declined. The middle class expanded to an estimated 29 percent of the population by 1970. From 1960 to 1980 illiteracy dropped from 35 to 15 percent of the population, infant mortality was reduced from seventy-eight to seventy per thousand live births, and average life expectancy rose from fifty-five to sixty-four years. Clearly, the quality of life for many Mexicans—even in isolated rural areas— did improve during this period, although several other Latin American countries (Chile, Colombia, Costa Rica, Cuba, Ecuador, El Salvador, and Venezuela) achieved higher rates of improvement on indicators of social well-being than did Mexico during the same period.

There was, however, a dark side to Mexico's "economic miracle." From 1950 to the mid-1970s, ownership of land and capital (stocks, bonds, time deposits) became increasingly concentrated. Personal income inequality also increased, at a time when, given Mexico's level of development, the national income distribution should have been shifting toward greater equality. Indeed, Mexico appears to have had a higher overall concentration of income in the mid-1970s than it had in 1910, before the outbreak of the Revolution.[88] By 1977 the poorest 70 percent of Mexican families received only 24 percent of all disposable income, while the richest

---

[88]See David Felix, "Income Distribution Trends in Mexico and the Kuznets Curve," in *Brazil and Mexico: Patterns in Late Development*, ed. Sylvia A. Hewlett and Richard S. Weinert (Philadelphia: Institute for the Study of Human Issues, 1982), 265-316.

30 percent of families received 76 percent of income. A government survey indicates that the income distribution became slightly more equal between 1977 and 1984, but this may have been due to the extraordinarily large number of new jobs created during the oil boom years of 1978-81, most of which were eliminated during the severe economic contraction of 1982-88.[89]

Other social indicators mirrored the trends in income distribution. By 1975 nearly 60 percent of Mexico's people did not consume the minimum diet needed to prevent nutritional diseases. Only half of the children who started primary school finished it (barely 20 percent in the most impoverished rural areas). Among the dwellings included in the 1980 census, nearly half had no sewage connections, 29 percent had no piped water, and 25 percent had no electricity. In Mexico City, 42 percent of the population was found to be living in squatter settlements.

On every indicator of economic opportunity and social well-being, there were also vast disparities among Mexico's regions and between rural and urban areas. Unemployment and underemployment were concentrated overwhelmingly in the rural population, and the rate of infant mortality in rural areas was nearly 50 percent higher than the national average. The central urban core (the Mexico City metropolitan area) had a per capita income that was double the national average, while the country's poorest, predominantly rural regions—containing nearly half the national population—had a smaller per capita income in 1970 than the central core region had in 1900.

The policies and investment preferences of Mexico's postrevolutionary governments contributed much to this pattern of inegalitarian development. At minimum, the public policies pursued since 1940 failed to counteract the wealth-concentrating effects of private market forces. And evidence is strong that some government investments and policies actually reinforced these effects. For example, during most of the post-1940 period, government tax and credit policies have worked primarily to the advantage of the country's large-scale agribusiness and industrial entrepreneurs. Government expenditures for social security, public health, and education remained relatively low by international standards. By the late 1970s Mexico was still allocating a smaller share of its central government budget to social services than countries like Bolivia, Brazil, Chile, and Panama. The slowness with which basic

[89]Data from the National Survey of Household Income and Expenditures (1984), analyzed in Fernando Cortés and Rosa María Rubalcava, "Equidad via reducción: La distribución del ingreso en México, 1977-1984" (unpublished manuscript, Center for U.S.-Mexican Studies, University of California, San Diego, June 1990).

social services were extended to the bulk of the population in Mexico was a direct consequence of the government's policy of keeping inflation low by concentrating public expenditures on subsidies and infrastructure for private industry, rather than social programs.

Even during the period from 1970 to 1982, when "populist" policies were allegedly in vogue and government revenues were expanding rapidly because of the oil export boom, public spending for programs like health and social security remained roughly constant in real per capita terms.[90] The economic crisis that erupted in 1982, after an unprecedented run-up in Mexico's domestic and externally held debt, made it impossible to maintain even that level of government commitment to social well-being. By 1986 debt service was consuming well over half of the total federal government budget (see figure 8), necessitating deep cuts in spending for health, education, consumer subsidies, and job-creating public investments. Social welfare expenditures per capita fell to 1974 levels.

The residue of the economic crisis and austere government budgets of the 1980s is an even more acute social crisis. Minimum real wages fell by 66 percent between 1980 and 1990. By 1987, according to the government's own statistics, more than half of Mexico's total population fell below the official poverty line, and more than 20 percent were living in what the government defines as "extreme poverty."[91] As the "lost decade" of the 1980s ended, some ten million Mexicans were suffering from what the government calls "critical" nutritional deficiencies.

The current government's "neoliberal" economic development model stresses the need to give much freer rein to market forces in order to attract more private investment (especially foreign capital), which is needed to push up Mexico's rate of economic growth. Spending on social programs like PRONASOL has increased each year since 1989, but the government argues that a significant increase in economic growth is the only way to make a major dent in Mexico's massive social deficit. Critics charge that "leaving it to the market," through such policies as reducing or eliminating government price subsidies for basic consumer goods and shrinking the role of the state as an employer, can only worsen

---

[90]Peter Ward, *Welfare Politics in Mexico: Papering Over the Cracks* (London: Allen and Unwin, 1986), 9-10, 135-36.

[91]John Sheahan, *Conflict and Change in Mexican Economic Strategy: Implications for Mexico and Latin America* (La Jolla, Calif.: Center for U.S.-Mexican Studies, University of California, San Diego, forthcoming); and Luis Donaldo Colosio, "Un nuevo partido," *Examen* [PRI] 2:13 (June 15, 1990): 4.

Figure 8

Mexican Government Budgets
1979-1989

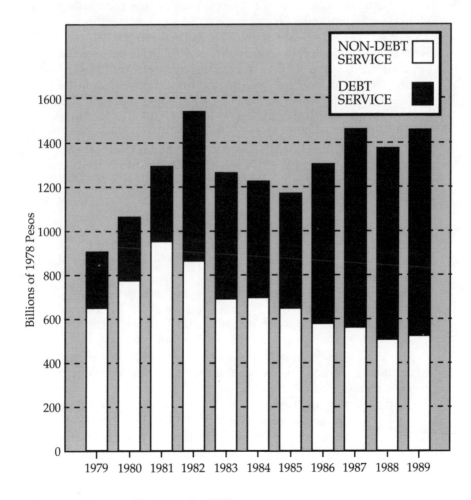

Source: Centeno, *Mexico in the 1990s.*

the social crisis. Moreover, Mexico's experience with rapid economic growth during the "miracle" years suggests that without strong, sustained government action to correct for market failures and reduce inequality, income concentration will continue unabated.

POPULATION AND EMPLOYMENT

The government can be credited with a major role in reducing Mexico's rate of population growth, which by the early 1970s was 3.5 percent per year—one of the world's highest growth rates. From the early nineteenth century through the 1930s the Mexican population expanded at a relatively moderate rate. Around 1940 it began a sharp upward climb, as advances in public health reduced the mortality rate while the birth rate remained constant. The population grew from 20 million in 1940 to 35 million in 1960 to at least 81 million in 1990.[92] Entering office in 1970 with an endorsement of the traditional pronatalist policy of the Mexican government, President Luis Echeverría was convinced three years later by his advisers that the huge resources that would be needed to feed, educate, and provide productive employment for a population doubling in size every twenty years were beyond Mexico's possibilities. A nationwide family planning program was launched in 1974, and within a few years the birth rate had begun to fall noticeably. By 1990, Mexico's population was growing at somewhere between 1.9 and 2.1 percent per year.

Regardless of Mexico's recent success in limiting new births, the country's labor force is still growing by about 3.5 percent annually because of the high birth rates of the 1960s and early '70s. This growth rate adds one million persons to the ranks of job seekers each year. Since nearly half of the nation's population is under the age of sixteen, the demand for new jobs will remain strong well into the next century.

Unfortunately, the explosive growth of Mexico's labor force has coincided in recent years with a period of stagnation in job creation. By 1986, open unemployment had risen to an estimated 15.4 percent. The official unemployment rate fell below 6 percent in 1990, as the recovery from the economic crisis of the 1980s gained momentum; but both of these statistics greatly understate the magnitude of Mexico's employment problem. The government considers a person employed if he or she works only one

---

[92]The official census count in 1990 was 81.1 million inhabitants, but this may have been affected by significant undercounting. Demographers estimate that the true population size in 1990 was about 84.9 million.

hour per week, and World Bank studies suggest that underemployment is a far more significant problem than open unemployment, affecting perhaps 25-35 percent of the economically active population.[93] Many of these people have taken refuge in the so-called informal economy, working as unlicensed street vendors (up to one million of them in the Mexico City metropolitan area alone), washing windshields at busy intersections, sewing garments in their homes, and performing a wide variety of other tasks outside of the "formal" sector. This underground economy accounted for an estimated 28-35 percent of Mexico's gross domestic product in 1986.[94] Much of Mexico's underemployment is also being exported to the United States through illegal immigration.

Perhaps the greatest deficiency of the post-1940 Mexican development strategy was the failure to develop an employment base adequate to absorb the labor force growth of the 1980s and 1990s. In the countryside, massive government investments in irrigation projects, "green revolution" technologies, infrastructure, and agricultural credit programs all benefited large producers far more than small farmers. This placed even greater capital resources in the hands of large landowners, who were able to mechanize their operations more rapidly. In agriculture as well as urban-based industry, government subsidies for acquisition of labor-saving machinery made it financially attractive for large-scale producers to substitute capital for labor.

An estimated 1.5 million jobs would have to be created annually until the year 2000 in order to absorb currently unemployed or severely underemployed Mexicans (the "backlog") and to provide employment opportunities for the new entrants into the labor force.[95] Job creation on that scale would require the Mexican economy to grow extremely fast (at least 7-8 percent per annum, in real terms), risking hyperinflation. Moreover, businesses would have to be compelled to use much more labor-intensive technologies, at a time when they are under considerable pressure from the government and the marketplace to become highly efficient, globally competitive exporters. In short, coming fully to grips with Mexico's employment problem at this time would conflict with some

93World Bank, *Mexico after the Oil Boom: Refashioning a Development Strategy* (Washington, D.C., June 1987).

94Centro de Estudios Económicos del Sector Privado, *La economía subterránea en México* (México, D.F.: CEESP, 1986).

95Leopoldo Solís, "Social Impact of the Economic Crisis," in *Mexico's Search for a New Development Strategy*, ed. Dwight S. Brothers and Adele E. Wick (Boulder, Colo.: Westview, 1990), 46.

of the key elements of the economic stabilization and restructuring project to which the government is committed.

FINANCING DEVELOPMENT AND CONTROLLING INFLATION

From 1940 to 1970, Mexico's public sector acquired an international reputation for sound, conservative monetary and fiscal policies. This conservative style of economic management, coupled with Mexico's long record of political stability, gave the country an attractive investment climate. By 1982 this image had been shattered; the public sector (and much of the private sector) was suffering from a deep liquidity crisis, and inflation had reached levels unheard of since the first decade of the Mexican Revolution, when paper currencies lost most of their value. What happened?

The basic difficulty was that the government had attempted to spend its way out of the social and economic problems that had accumulated since 1940, without paying the political cost that sweeping redistributive policies would have entailed. Instead, it attempted to expand the entire economic pie by enlarging the state's role as banker, entrepreneur, and employer. Throughout the period since 1940, and especially after 1970, Mexico's public sector expanded steadily while its revenue-raising capability lagged. The result was ever-larger government deficits, financed increasingly by borrowing abroad.

For most of the post-World War II period, Mexico's tax effort—its rate of taxation and its actual performance in collecting taxes—was among the lowest in the world. Officials feared that any major alteration in the tax structure would stampede domestic and foreign capital out of the country. Two modest attempts at tax reform, in 1964 and 1972, failed because of determined opposition from business elites. When the private sector refused to accede to higher taxes, the Echeverría administration opted for large-scale deficit financing, external indebtedness, and a huge increase in the money supply. The public sector itself was vastly enlarged, increasing the number of state-owned enterprises from 84 in 1970 to 845 in 1976. Fiscal restraint was finally forced on the government by depletion of its currency reserves in 1976.

Echeverría's successor, José López Portillo, at first attempted to reverse the trend toward larger government deficits, but the effort was abandoned when the treasury began to swell with oil export revenues. Again, the temptation was to address basic structural problems by further expanding the state sector, and López Portillo found it impossible to resist. Oil revenues seemed to be a guaranteed, limitless source of income for the government. Mexico borrowed heavily abroad, anticipating a steady rise in oil prices.

Although Mexico's long-term foreign debt (owed by both the government and private Mexican firms) had grown substantially during the Echeverría sexenio (from $12.1 billion in 1970 to $30.5 billion in 1976), the most rapid expansion occurred during López Portillo's "oil boom" administration. By the end of 1982, Mexico's external debt totaled nearly $82 billion, with annual interest payments of $16 billion (compared with $475 million paid to service the debt in 1970). In August 1982, the government was forced to suspend repayment of principal and begin a difficult renegotiation of the size and terms of the debt with Mexico's foreign creditors—the first of several such "restructurings," the most recent of which was completed in 1990. By the end of that year, Mexico had reduced its total long-term external debt to about $93 billion, but annual interest payments still totaled $11 billion—considerably more than Mexico earns from its oil exports in an average year.

Deficit financing, especially in the context of the overheated economy of the oil boom years, also touched off a burst of inflation. The average annual inflation rate rose from 15 percent during Echeverría's presidency (nearly triple the average rate during the 1940-70 period) to 36 percent under López Portillo and 91 percent in the de la Madrid sexenio (159 percent in 1987). Both the de la Madrid and Salinas administrations made reducing the inflation rate their top economic priority, but Salinas has been much more successful in bringing inflation under control than his predecessor. His principal instrument was price and wage controls, enforced by a formal, government/business-organized labor pact that has been renewed, with some adjustments, at 12-18 month intervals. This form of "shock" therapy for inflation has proven more successful in Mexico than in any other country where it has been applied, bringing the inflation rate down to the 20-30 percent range in 1989-90. The key to a successful economic stabilization program has been deep cuts in government spending coupled with unprecedented steps to boost revenues, including vigorous enforcement of the tax laws and the selling of hundreds of state-owned enterprises to private investors. Of the 1,171 state enterprises existing in 1982, only 344 had not been privatized or liquidated or were in progress of divestment by the end of 1990.[96] The Salinas administration has justified its policy of shrinking the

---

[96]Data from the Centro de Estudios Económicos del Sector Privado, Mexico City. See also Oscar Vera Ferrer, "The Political Economy of Privatization in Mexico," in *Privatization of Public Enterprises in Latin America*, ed. William Glade (San Francisco and San Diego: ICS Press/Center for U.S.-Mexican Studies, 1991), 35-57.

public sector by arguing that it is necessary to free up scarce resources, allowing the government to concentrate on meeting pressing social needs.

Mexico's Political Future: Transition to What?

The progressive breakdown of the one-party hegemonic political system in Mexico raises the question of what will replace it. Below we sketch four possible scenarios for Mexico's future political evolution, taking into account the already observable changes, the political system's historic propensity for adaptation to changing realities in its environment, and the array of international constraints now weighing so heavily on political decision-makers in Mexico.

IMMOBILISM

In this scenario, Mexico's ruling elite will prove unable to adapt constructively to the country's new political environment. Responses to widespread demands for democratization will be too slow, too tentative, and too narrowly constrained by the state to satisfy the groups now pressing for a political opening. Democratization from above, even if pushed strongly by a reform-minded president, is no longer a realistic possibility. Either the "dinosaurs" will triumph in the struggle for control of the PRI, or the party will be irrevocably split, with the old-style corporatists and the modernizing technocrats going their own separate ways, taking whatever supporters they can muster. Less and less encumbered by presidential authority, intra-elite conflict may produce a series of political impasses to which the regime may be unable to respond effectively.

With increased fragmentation of the ruling elite, little could be done to halt further atrophy of the PRI and its sectoral organizations. The sectoral leaders' weakness will make them even more defensive and resistant to reform. Rather than a Spanish-style, relatively smooth, low-conflict transition to democracy guided from above, Mexico will be condemned to a Polish-style transition, in which each change is the result of an open and prolonged confrontation with the opposition, which ends with the regime making concessions.

The deep and difficult-to-repair cleavages within Mexico's ruling elite over political reform alone could be sufficient to induce immobilism. The probability of such a scenario would be greatly increased, however, if the economic recovery stalls (perhaps due to a prolonged, worldwide recession) or if the stabilization pact breaks down, initiating a new inflationary spiral. Without vigorous, sustained economic growth, the government could not meet its social objectives; absolute poverty, malnutrition, unemployment, and inequality in wealth distribution would continue to increase. Renewed economic grievances would provoke an upsurge in anti-PRI protest voting in future elections, further stiffening the resolve of the regime's "dinosaurs" to block any further changes in the rules of electoral competition that could benefit the opposition.

The opposition forces presently arrayed against the incumbent regime themselves appear to suffer a degree of immobilism in developing their own economic and political projects, beyond simple protest of PRI fraud and criticism of government policies. On the right, the construction of an alternative "legitimacy" is complicated by the coincidence of many policy views and interests between the PANistas and the governing technocrats. On the left, both the most prominent national leaders and many of their supporters are none other than "the authentic children of the PRI."[97] The ruling technocrats' economic restructuring project may fail to produce the promised social benefits; but building a broad societal consensus around an alternative model—based on realistic assumptions about Mexico's options at home and abroad—could prove very difficult for the leftist opposition.

Among both leftist and rightist opponents of the regime, the challenges of portraying themselves as a credible alternative and defending their vote against PRI-government fraud will be complicated by infighting. A highly fractious and disorganized opposition will not be able to exert the strong pressure on PRI and government hard-liners that would be needed to move the authoritarian system more rapidly toward democracy. Even though the PRI will continue to deteriorate, no opposition party

97Barry Carr, "The Left and Its Potential Role in Political Change," in *Mexico's Alternative Political Futures*, ed. Cornelius, Gentleman, and Smith, 383.

will have the capacity to replace it in power, at least at the national level.

Immobilism in politics and public policy making—the kind of political stalemate or "politics of social draw" that have regularly beset countries like Argentina and Italy[98]—could not be sustained indefinitely in contemporary Mexico. The accumulation of unresolved social problems during the 1970s and '80s has been too great. The organized opposition to the regime is now too strong, and the recent changes in political consciousness among even unorganized segments of the Mexican population are irreversible—even if that consciousness now manifests itself in nonvoting. The current inability of opposition forces to clearly articulate and advance counterclaims may provide breathing space for the PRI-government apparatus, but this advantage is likely to be fleeting. In short, the "immobilism" scenario would be a prescription for chronic crisis and a gradual unraveling of the coalition that has governed Mexico since the 1930s.

POLITICAL CLOSURE

In this scenario, pressures for hardening of the regime will mount during Salinas's term, forcing him to abandon all attempts at political reform, in the interest of assuring a minimum level of elite cohesion and/or maintaining social order. Political retrenchment could result from a failure of the neoliberal economic model favored by Salinas and the technocrats in his cabinet to produce a strong economic recovery. Thus, the government would have to rely increasingly on authoritarian means to impose its policies amid a continuing decline in living standards and job opportunities. Some see political hardening as a requirement of a *successful* neoliberal economic project, because of its high social costs. Reflecting on the implementation of this model in Chile during the 1970s, they predict the "Chileanization" of Mexico—a shift toward a significantly more authoritarian style of governance, with less respect for individual liberties and a rising level of government

---

[98]As described by Torcuato Di Tella, "Argentina has been stagnating for many years as a result of political stalemate. The various contenders for power simply can't liquidate each other, though they have been trying hard for the last three decades. At times one or the other of those groups seems on the verge of succeeding, but somehow society resists strongly, and a 'social draw' is reestablished. Each group has just enough power to veto the projects originated by the others, but none can muster the strength to run the country as it would like." (Torcuato S. Di "An Introduction to the Argentine System," in *Political Power in Latin Ameri Confrontations*, ed. Richard R. Fagen and Wayne A. Cornelius [Englew N.J.: Prentice-Hall, 1970], 108.)

coercion. Unlike the Chilean case, there would be no overt interruption of constitutional processes, but rather a creeping, rightist coup d'état within the regime itself, as the Soviet Union now appears to be undergoing.

Recourse to coercion would be even more likely in the event that opposition parties try to provoke social turmoil. Besieged political authorities, increasingly overwhelmed by events that seem to be spinning out of their control, may respond with mass repression. Even in less dramatic circumstances, old-guard PRI leaders and government bureaucrats who feel threatened by the emergence of new popular movements and organizations outside of existing corporatist structures may press for a "closing down" response. Since the PRI seems to have lost the capacity to incorporate such movements, there may be a strong temptation to simply repress them rather than try to build strategic alliances with them.

Increasing repression would be very costly for the regime's legitimacy, however, both at home and abroad. Indiscriminate use of coercion would divide the ruling political elite even more deeply than neoliberal economic policies have done. The country would become increasingly ungovernable, with the proliferation of bitter, unmediated conflicts. Foreign investment would be frightened away by the prospect of destabilization, and domestic capital would again flee the country. The loss of private-sector confidence would effectively prevent the modernizing technocrats from carrying through their economic restructuring project. Moreover, it would be very difficult for the United States to live with a much more authoritarian regime in Mexico, thereby impeding major initiatives like a North American free trade agreement, which is central to the Mexican government's new export-oriented development strategy. For all these reasons, it seems likely that any hardening of the regime would stop well short of overt repression. Both the economic and political costs of a harsh, authoritarian closure would be prohibitively high.

ORITARIANISM WITH SELECTIVE

Mexico's political elite to emergent
getic revival and remodeling of the
rebuilt on a new set of organizations
dernization-of-authoritarianism" scebuild the PRI along territorial lines and
rough democratization of the party's
rocess would be successful—within its

4

carefully defined limits. Given the relatively low probability of a permanent, unified opposition party of the left in Mexico and the rightist opposition's limitations in expanding its current largely middle- and upper-class social base, a modernized PRI would not confront a serious opposition threat to its control of the presidency or most state governorships. The result would be more acceptable PRI candidates (at least at the municipal level), perhaps more lively debate within the PRI over public policy issues, but no truly effective opposition outside of the ruling party. The government would also take steps to expand freedom of expression (e.g., by relaxing controls on the electronic media) and to curb human rights abuses by the police and caciques.

To make the PRI more competitive against the opposition and thereby reduce the necessity to resort to blatant and disruptive electoral fraud, a modernization of authoritarianism could be combined with a policy of "selective populism." Pockets of popular discontent can be bought off with limited material benefits channeled through programs like National Solidarity, which also help the regime to maintain its socially "progressive" credentials and preempt leftist opposition groups.

This kind of carefully modulated, incremental, elite-initiated political liberalization would not necessarily pave the way for genuine democratization. There is virtually no evidence to suggest that the majority of PRI leaders accept the idea that their party will cease to be the "party of the state," much less cease to be the governing party. They may endorse a political opening, but without real risk of losing power.

LIMITED POWER SHARING: THE INDIAN CONGRESS PARTY MODEL

Recognizing the importance and durability of subnational variations in support for the PRI and its opposition, realists in the PRI-government apparatus may seek to transform the political system along the lines of the postindependence Indian experience. Before they took power in 1988, some of Salinas's more reform-minded advisers sometimes cited the Indian Congress Party model as an acceptable and even desirable outcome of Mexico's transition from a hegemonic one-party system.

Acceptance of the Indian model implies a willingness to surrender control of municipal and state governments *routinely* to the rightist or leftist opposition in their regional strongholds, in the interest of staying in power at the national level. Under such a system, elections at the state and local levels in most parts of the country would be considerably more competitive than they have been, even in recent years. The PRI would retain control of the presidency and the Congress (as long as it won at least 35 percent of the votes in national elections). However, with truly competitive elections being held in a larger number of states and localities, the PRI's future presidential candidates would probably be elected by a plurality rather than a majority of the vote and the ruling party would be unlikely to win the two-thirds majority of seats in the Chamber of Deputies that is needed to amend the Constitution.

A shift from PRI hegemony at all levels to a situation of continued PRI domination of national politics combined with real, multiparty competition at the local and state levels would ensure that political institutions at those levels would be considerably more responsive to the citizenry than in the present system. The level of mass political participation would rise, and elections would function once again as an important social and political safety valve. Finally, the need to become competitive in state and local elections would serve as a spur for internal reform and rejuvenation of the PRI itself, without risking the party's continued control of the truly important positions in the system.

A move to adopt the Congress Party model would provoke strong resistance from entrenched, subnational PRI bosses. Elections for state and municipal offices held since mid-1988 in several parts of the country—most notably Baja California Norte—have been marked by sharp, public disputes between the national PRI organization and the party's state and local leaders, who are committed, not to sharing power, but to avoiding defeat at any cost. As Mexican political scientist Federico Estévez has observed, lower-echelon PRI officials "no longer align themselves automatically with dictates from the center."[99] The conflict of interest between such leaders and the modernizing national political elite is one of the most fundamental obstacles to a political opening that assures both the PRI and its opposition a share of power.

After the momentous developments of 1987-88, it was widely assumed that none of the principal actors in the Mexican political system could return to "business as usual." This conventional wisdom has been upset by Carlos Salinas's determination to complete the restructuring of the economy at the expense of more rapid political liberalization. Salinas and his most probable succes-

---

[99]Federico Estévez, "Salinastroika Opens a Hornets' Nest," *Los Angeles Times*, July 15, 1990.

sors know, however, that a serious opening of the political system cannot be postponed indefinitely, and that the PRI must be prepared for a period of greater political competition. They want to avoid another situation like 1988, in which the PRI's hold on the presidency may be seriously threatened by a wave of protest voting and the charisma of an opposition candidate. But they are unwilling to tear the PRI apart in order to reform it.

The Mexican public and most professional analysts of Mexican politics remain skeptical that the PRI can be rebuilt to function as a real political party, able and willing to compete everywhere for power on relatively equal terms with the opposition. Central control of the far-flung PRI apparatus, of its "mass" organizations and local caciques is weakening, and it remains to be seen whether Salinas or any future PRI president can succeed in imposing drastic political reform on a resistant base.

Strong external pressure will continue to be needed to keep the reformist impulse alive within the PRI-government apparatus. Thus, the outcome of the political transition that began to unfold so dramatically in 1988 still depends to a very large extent on what happens with the opposition, especially to the left of the PRI. To influence that outcome, opposition forces would have to consolidate themselves into coherent, well-institutionalized political parties with credible alternative policies.

It is also possible that Mexico's ruling elite, with its vaunted pragmatism and flexibility intact, can muddle through a middle ground, in which there is no return to pre-1988 hegemonic control by the PRI, but a generally weak party system; elections that are more competitive, but whose results continue to lack credibility; a president who must operate under new limits, but who remains firmly in control of the ruling party and the Congress; no recourse to widespread repression, but persisting human rights abuses in certain parts of the country; and no real movement toward unfettered, Western-style democracy.[100]

---

[100]Many of the factors that make this kind of hybrid, semi-authoritarian regime the most probable short-to-medium-term outcome of Mexico's political transition are analyzed in Lorenzo Meyer, "México: Los límites de la democratización neo-liberal" (paper presented at the Research Seminar on Mexico and U.S.-Mexican Relations, Center for U.S.-Mexican Studies, University of California, San Diego, May 15, 1991). An abridged version of this paper was published in *Nexos* 163 (July 1991): 25-34.

Selected Bibliography

Alvarado Mendoza, Arturo, ed. *Electoral Patterns and Perspectives in Mexico.* La Jolla, Calif.: Center for U.S.-Mexican Studies, University of California, San Diego, 1987.

Bailey, John J. *Governing Mexico: The Statecraft of Crisis Management.* New York: St. Martin's, 1988.

Barkin, David. *Distorted Development: Mexico in the World Economy.* Boulder, Colo.: Westview, 1990.

Bilateral Commission on the Future of U.S.-Mexican Relations. *The Challenge of Interdependence: Mexico and the United States.* Lanham, Md.: University Press of America, 1989.

Camp, Roderic A. *Entrepreneurs and Politics in Twentieth Century Mexico.* New York: Oxford University Press, 1989.

Cornelius, Wayne A. *Politics and the Migrant Poor in Mexico City.* Stanford, Calif.: Stanford University Press, 1975.

Cornelius, Wayne A., Judith Gentleman, and Peter H. Smith, eds. *Mexico s Alternative Political Futures.* La Jolla, Calif.: Center for U.S.-Mexican Studies, University of California, San Diego, 1989.

Cypher, James M. *State and Capital in Mexico: Development Policy since 1940.* Boulder, Colo.: Westview, 1990.

Eckstein, Susan. *The Poverty of Revolution: The State and the Urban Poor in Mexico.* Princeton, N.J.: Princeton University Press, 1988.

Fagen, Richard R., and William S. Tuohy. *Politics and Privilege in a Mexican City.* Stanford, Calif.: Stanford University Press, 1972.

Foweraker, Joe, and Ann L. Craig, eds. *Popular Movements and Political Change in Mexico.* Boulder, Colo.: Lynne Rienner, 1990.

Gentleman, Judith, ed. *Mexican Politics in Transition.* Boulder, Colo.: Westview, 1987.

González de la Rocha, Mercedes, and Agustín Escobar Latapí, eds. *Social Responses to Mexico s Economic Crisis of the 1980s.* La Jolla, Calif.: Center for U.S.-Mexican Studies, University of California, San Diego, 1991.

Green, Rosario, and Peter H. Smith, series eds. *Dimensions of U.S.-Mexican Relations.* 5 vols. La Jolla, Calif.: Center for U.S.-Mexican Studies, University of California, San Diego, 1989.

Knight, Alan, *The Mexican Revolution.* 2 vols. London: Cambridge University Press, 1986.

Levy, Daniel, and Gabriel Székely. *Mexico: Paradoxes of Stability and Change,* 2d ed. Boulder, Colo.: Westview, 1987.

Maxfield, Sylvia. *Governing Capital: International Finance and Mexican Politics.* Ithaca, N.Y.: Cornell University Press, 1990.

Middlebrook, Kevin, ed. *Unions, Workers, and the State in Mexico.* La Jolla, Calif.: Center for U.S.-Mexican Studies, University of California, San Diego, 1991.

Ronfeldt, David, ed. *The Modern Mexican Military: A Reassessment.* La Jolla, Calif.: Center for U.S.-Mexican Studies, University of California, San Diego, 1984.

Saragoza, Alex M. *The Monterrey Elite and the Mexican State.* Austin: University of Texas Press, 1988.

Smith, Peter H. *Labyrinths of Power: Political Recruitment in Twentieth-Century Mexico.* Princeton, N.J.: Princeton University Press, 1979.

Ward, Peter M. *Mexico City: The Production and Reproduction of an Urban Environment.* London: Belhaven Press, 1990.

——. *Welfare Politics in Mexico: Papering Over the Cracks.* London: Allen and Unwin, 1986.

Wilkie, James W. *The Mexican Revolution: Federal Expenditure and Social Change since 1910.* 2d ed. Berkeley: University of California Press, 1970.

About the Authors

Wayne A. Cornelius is the Gildred Professor of Political Science and U.S.-Mexican Relations, and Director of the Center for U.S.-Mexican Studies, at the University of California, San Diego. He specializes in Mexican politics and the political economy of international labor migration. His publications include *Politics and the Migrant Poor in Mexico City* (1975) and *Mexico's Alternative Political Futures* (co-edited with Judith Gentleman and Peter H. Smith, 1989).

Ann L. Craig is Associate Professor of Political Science at the University of California, San Diego. Her publications include *The First Agraristas: An Oral History of a Mexican Agrarian Reform Movement* (1983) and *Popular Movements and Political Change in Mexico* (co-edited with Joe Foweraker, 1990).